STUDY GUIDE

For The

Florida Corrections Officer's Certification Examination

William G. Doerner, Ph.D.
School of Criminology and Criminal Justice
The Florida State University
Tallahassee, Florida 32306-2025

and

Charles W. Rushing, M.A.
Pat Thomas Criminal Justice Training Academy
Route 1, Box 3250
Havana, Florida 32333

Pineapple Press, Inc.
Sarasota, Florida

Bill Doerner and Chuck Rushing at the Police Academy

Inquiries should be addressed to:

Pineapple Press, Inc.
P.O. Box 3889
Sarasota, Florida 34230

www.pineapplepress.com

Library of Congress Cataloging-in-Publication Data

Doerner, William G.
Study guide for the Florida corrections officer's certification examination / William G. Doerner and Charles W. Rushing.–2nd ed.
p. cm.
ISBN 1-56164-279-7 (pbk. : alk. paper)
1. Correctional personnel–Florida–Examinations, questions, etc. 2. Corrections–Florida–Examinations, questions, etc. 3. Corrections–Vocational guidance–Florida. 4. Employment tests–Florida. I. Rushing, Charles W., 1939- . II. Title.
HV9475.F6D64 1997
365' .64'076–dc21

97-28396

Second Edition
10 9 8 7 6 5 4 3 2 1

Design by Carol Tornatore
Printed in the United States of America

CONTENTS

CHAPTER 1

The Florida Corrections Officer Certification Examination

Mission Statement

Florida Criminal Justice Standards & Training Commission. To ensure that all citizens of Florida are served by criminal justice officers who are ethical, qualified, and well trained.

Introduction

Congratulations on completing the basic recruit training program at the corrections academy! If you were to sit back for a moment and reminisce about what you have accomplished so far, you might conclude that your career plans are progressing very nicely and without any major hitches. As tempting as it might seem, though, now is not the time to slack off or become complacent with your career goals. The next hurdle awaits you. It is the Florida Corrections Officer Certification Examination.

Figures released by the Florida Department of Law Enforcement (FDLE) reveal that a number of people who graduate from the corrections academy do not score a passing grade on the statewide certification examination. In order to appreciate just how serious this lack of performance can be, keep one important thing in mind. FDLE does not permit anybody who fails this qualifying test to work as a sworn corrections officer within the state. No matter how outstanding your academy grades were, how terrific your credentials are, or how many job offers you may have pending, they are all insignificant at this point. You *must* pass the certification examination to launch your corrections career.

Given the overwhelming importance of this test, what should your next step be? Plan and prepare. If there is any one lesson that you should have absorbed during your academy days, it is that corrections officers need to plan and to prepare before taking any action. This same sage advice applies to your situation. You need to plan and to prepare for the most important test of your corrections career.

This study guide is intended to help you get ready for the corrections officer certification examination. The goal behind this manual is to supplement, not replace, the lessons you derived from your academy training. The notes you took at the academy and the materials that instructors distributed during class represent the foundation of your professional education. The questions and exercises that appear in this handbook are designed to sharpen those skills. Contrary to wishful thinking, there is no shortcut to studying for the exam, and there is simply no substitute for your own hard work.

The Criminal Justice Standards and Training (CJS&T) Commission at FDLE has prepared a booklet called "Applicant Information Handbook" for those persons interested in the Florida Corrections Officer Certification Examination. Copies are available from your local training academy at no cost. Before we delve right into the exam itself, though, it may be worthwhile to take a few moments and see how FDLE has been changing the face of corrections in Florida.

Background

The State of Florida has displayed a keen interest in upgrading the quality of its corrections officers for quite a while. In 1967, the state legislature enacted Florida Statutes Chapter 943 which established minimum standards for all sworn personnel. This new law spelled out various entrance requirements that each recruit had to satisfy to become licensed or certified as a corrections officer in Florida. Probably the most visible feature was that all recruits were required to attend a state-sponsored corrections academy as part of their occupational preparation.

Over the years, the Florida CJS&T Commission developed a standardized basic recruit curriculum which you have experienced already. These lesson plans outline different training topics, specify the number of instructional hours devoted to various topics, and include learning goals to guide academy instructors when preparing lesson plans. Despite such systematic oversight, this approach met with mixed success. One complaint that surfaced regularly was that many corrections academy graduates displayed inferior skills. The wash-out rate that many agencies registered during the initial rookie training phase made administrators wonder what kind of learning and skills development were taking place during the preservice academy instruction. These objections forced the Commission to take a closer look at preservice corrections training in Florida.

The latest wrinkle in the quest to place only the most qualified people in uniform took effect on July 1, 1993. Florida now requires all correctional officer candidates to pass a state board examination after completing the academy training module. A passing score on this four-hour state examination is a prerequisite to becoming certified as a corrections officer. Agencies are barred from placing anybody who fails this test into a sworn position.

As one might expect, test performances vary throughout the state. Some academies post much higher pass rates than do other locations. As time goes by, it would not be unreasonable to expect additional variation from one academy to another and from one class to the next within the same training facility. As a result, assembling a study guide that would help Florida corrections academy graduates prepare for the statewide certification exam seemed to us to be a reasonable and sensible direction to take.

Examination Eligibility

As we mentioned before, Florida law does not allow the CJS&T Commission to certify academy graduates as corrections officers until these novices pass the qualifying exam. Only those persons who fit into one of the following categories can take this test:

- Anyone who has completed a Commission-approved corrections basic recruit training program within the past four years;
- Anyone who has completed a Commission-approved corrections cross-over training program within the past four years;
- Anyone seeking reinstatement after a four year break in service who has completed the required pre-exam training;
- Anyone who has served as a corrections officer in another state or federal capacity for at least one year, has completed a basic corrections training program similar to the Florida curriculum, and who has completed the required pre-exam training.

The Exam Application

A person who wishes to take the corrections officer certification examination must submit an application to the CJS&T Commission along with a cashier's check or money order in the amount of $75 payable to the "Criminal Justice Training Trust Fund." Personal checks or cash are not acceptable.

The application itself is a computer scan sheet titled "Application for Officer Certification Examination" and is available at your local training academy. Applicants must insert the appropriate codes in the designated spaces and darken the corresponding letter or number in the column underneath the entry with a number 2 lead pencil. The application asks for such information as name, social security, examination type (corrections, correctional probation, or law enforcement), type of training completed, name of the training academy, graduation date from the training academy, date you are requesting to take the exam, and a number of other items. The instructions specifically remind applicants to contact their training school, not the Florida Department of Law Enforcement, for test scheduling information. Tests are administered every month at several different locations throughout the state.

Once the application is complete, the applicant must sign and date the form. The application and $75 test fee should be mailed to the following address:

> ATTN: Division of Staff Services
> Bureau of Finance & Accounting
> Florida Department of Law Enforcement
> Post Office Box 1489
> Tallahassee, Florida 32302-1489

Checklist for Submitting the Exam Application
First-Time Exam Takers:

__ Complete the application and shade in the appropriate oval within each column.
__ Sign the application.
__ Include $75 cashier's check or money order payable to the "Criminal Justice Training Fund." Personal checks, cash, or credit cards will not be honored.
__ Include written request for special conditions should any apply.

Repeat Exam Takers:

__ Complete the application and shade in the appropriate oval within each column.
__ Sign the application.
__ Include $75 cashier's check or money order payable to the "Criminal Justice Training Fund." Personal checks, cash, or credit cards will not be honored.
__ Include written request for special conditions should any apply.
__ Include a copy of the grade notification letter for the last examination.
__ Include a signed statement from the training school that you have undergone retraining if this your third time taking the exam.

Mail the application at least 45 days prior to the exam to:

ATTN: Division of Staff Services
Bureau of Finance & Accounting
Florida Department of Law Enforcement
Post Office Box 1489
Tallahassee, Florida 32302-1489

Applications that are not properly completed, are not signed, do not include any required documents if requesting a retake, or are not accompanied with the exam fee will be returned to the applicant unprocessed. Any such oversights may mean that you may not be eligible to take the exam on the day you are requesting. Obviously, it is very important to take a few minutes to double-check your application. Use the application checklist that appears to the left to ensure that your package is complete.

Exam Contents

The Florida Corrections Certification Examination consists of 300 multiple-choice questions which are arranged in five sections. The questions themselves come from the basic recruit training curriculum followed at the corrections academy. The following chart outlines what appears within each section of the test. The course designators and titles correspond to specific portions of your academy train-

Outline of the Florida Corrections Officer Certification Examination

Part 1	Part 2	Part 3	Part 4	Part 5
CJD 770 Legal 1	CJD 773 Interpersonal Skills I	CJD 752 Correctional Operations	CJD 750 Interpersonal Skills II	CJD 704 Defensive Tactics
CJD 771 Legal 2			CJD 772 Communications	CJD 705 Weapons
				CJD 254 Medical First Responder
				CJD 741 Emergency Preparedness

ing. As you might guess, your notebook and other learning materials that you accumulated during the basic recruit course will serve as invaluable study materials during your preparation. Refer to them often!

Part One of the exam deals with such topics as ethics, the criminal justice system, legal terms, offense classification, the criminal code, constitutional law, search and seizure, juvenile procedures, traffic laws, and the like. Part Two concentrates on interviewing, interrogation, report writing, radio and telephone procedures, crisis intervention, domestic violence, crime prevention, and special needs of different groups such as the elderly, juveniles, mentally handicapped, and physically handicapped persons. The third section addresses investigative procedures, crime scene processing, fingerprinting, and other related aspects. Part Four includes such considerations as patrol practices for routine and high risk situations, officer survival, pursuit strategies, crowd control, and the like. The last section contains defensive tactics, physical restraint, prisoner transport, weapons familiarization, vehicle operations, traffic stops, crash scene procedures, and emergency medical procedures.

The questions that are presented throughout this study guide are derived from the goals and objectives that the Florida CJS&T Commission specifies in the course guide for the basic recruit training program. Every effort has been taken to ensure that the practice items reflect topics that are covered at the academy. As a result, this manual is to designed to complement and to reinforce the training that you have received already.

The Day of the Exam

After the CJS&T Commission processes your application, you will be notified as to the date, time, and location of the testing. The CJS&T requires you to be at the test site one hour prior to the scheduled beginning time. Late arrivals cannot be accommodated. Tardy persons will be denied access to the examination room and will forfeit the test fee.

To gain admission into the testing site, you must present the following three items:

- admission slip the CJS&T mailed back to you after processing your test application;
- a driver's license, state identification card, or a picture I.D. issued by a state agency;
- the "Certification of Completion" issued after you graduated from the basic recruit training program at the corrections academy *or* a signed statement from your training school director verifying that you have completed the required training program.

Should you forget to bring any one of these three items, you will not be allowed to take the examination.

To keep the examination room sterile, test-takers cannot bring any backpacks, fanny packs, briefcases, books, bags, purses, or any other satchels into the test site. Any personal items or supplies that you intend to carry into the testing room must be placed inside a clear plastic bag which is no larger than eight-and-a-half by eleven inches, the size of a regular notebook page. You should bring several sharpened number 2 lead pencils to the test since ball-point or felt-tip pens cannot be used.

Test-takers are not allowed to carry weapons, cameras, tape recorders, calculators, wristwatch calculators, computers, beepers, radios, telephones, books, reference materials, notes, dictionaries, thesauruses, spelling aids, or other items into the examination room. Food, drinks, and smoking are not permitted inside the examination room. You may bring a sweater or jacket with you in case the air conditioning is cooler than you like. However, hats or caps are not permitted.

Anybody who violates these restrictions, engages in cheating, impersonates a test-taker, retains an impersonator to take the exam on his or her behalf, reproduces or reconstructs any portion of the exam, distributes or receives or possesses an unauthorized copy of a certification exam, or behaves in any other questionable manner may be subject to sanctions. That penalty can include being declared ineligible to take the examination for a period of up to five years.

The Examination Administrator will issue a set of instructions and will distribute test materials at the appropriate times. Listen carefully to these guidelines and be sure to read all the directions carefully!

Test-Taking Tips

Probably one of the more important things you can do is to approach the certification examination with several strategies in mind. One thing you may want to do is to skip over questions that you find difficult. There is no requirement that you complete all the items in their numerical order. One rule of thumb, then, would be to answer all the questions that you are absolutely sure of, skip the others, and then return to these more difficult questions later. Double-check to be certain that the answer you bubble in on the scan sheet corresponds to the question number on the test. Marking the answer for question five in the spot reserved for question six will be of little benefit.

When you go back to the questions you did not answer the first time through the test, start crossing out any answers that do not apply. Sometimes you might know what the answer is not. In some instances, this strategy may reveal the appropriate choice by default.

Another thing you want to watch out for is not to forget to answer any of the questions. If you can eliminate some possible answers, do so. Making an educated guess from the remaining possible answers will enhance the probability of picking the correct answer. Remember, if you do not answer a question, you will not be able to gain credit for a correct response on that item.

Examination Results

The CJS&T Commission makes every effort to send your official grade notification letter within thirty days after you have taken the examination. However, if more than thirty days have elapsed and you still have not received your results, contact CJS&T to determine the reason for the delay. In addition to receiving scores that reflect the percentage of correct answers on each section, there will be either "yes" or "no" marks under the mastery level heading. A "yes" indicates you passed that section of the examination. A "no" means that you have failed that section of the examination.

If you have passed all five sections of the examination, you are eligible for certification. Should you fail one or more sections, you must wait ninety days to retake that portion of the examination. A new exam application must be submitted at least forty-five days prior to the test administration date. Should you fail the same section again, you must retake the courses listed under that portion of the test. You are eligible to retake that section of the exam after you finish this remedial course work. When you apply to retake the exam, you will need to include a "Certificate of Completion" or a statement from the training school documenting the retraining.

The CJS&T Commission is emphatic about the manner in which it relays test grades. Test scores cannot be released over the telephone, faxed, nor sent to a different address than what appears on your original application. Similarly, the CJS&T will not make your individual test results available to any outside source without your written authorization. Should your name or your address change after sending in the exam application, you must submit an "Address/Name Change Form" with the corrected information to the CJS&T.

Now let's get started with your preparation!

CHAPTER 2

Legal Aspects of Corrections

Chapter Overview

This portion of your preparation for the Florida Corrections Officer Certification Examination focuses upon your knowledge of Florida criminal law, constitutional law, and criminal justice procedures. As you work through the multiple-choice questions in this section, you will notice there are two distinct types of formats presented for your use. You will encounter both kinds of presentations on the certification examination.

The first style may be called "factual questions." These items concentrate on the actual contents of various Florida criminal statutes and other legal information. They may involve definitions, a recognition of different elements, or may deal with particular portions of an actual Florida criminal statute or constitutional practice.

The second series of questions concern "hypothetical situations." You will be given a set of facts surrounding an event, just like what a corrections officer might encounter in the field. You will then be asked to classify the incident as to the type of a crime this situation describes and whether the crime is a misdemeanor or a felony. As you can see, this portion of the test preparation quizzes your ability to apply your textbook knowledge of Florida laws to concrete situations.

The questions that appear in this section were chosen to reflect the goals and objectives that guide the corrections academy training program. You should follow several steps in order to master these materials. First, you should familiarize yourself with the Florida Statutes that pertain to criminal law and constitutional aspects *before* responding to the practice questions. Read over the appropriate Florida Statutes. Next, review your lecture notes from the academy. Then, focus on mastering the "factual questions" sections. An answer sheet listing the correct answers appears after the last question. Finally, work your way through the "hypothetical scenario" questions. An answer key appears at the end of this section so that you can check your progress. If your response differs from what appears in the answer key, you may want to go back and compare the legal aspects with the characteristics of the event.

By the time you complete this section, you should have a firm understanding of the following legal topics and Florida criminal statutes:

- Ethical and Professional Behavior
- Criminal Justice Standards and Training Commission
- History of Corrections
- Criminal Justice System Components
- Philosophies of Corrections
- Probation, Parole and Community Control
- Inmate Rights and Responsibilities
- Privileged Communication
- Correctional Officer Rights and Responsibilities
- History and Evolution of Laws
- Classification of Offenses
- Elements of a Crime
- Intent
- Parties to a Crime
- Civil and Criminal Liability
- Bribery
- Perjury
- Subpoena

- Court Rules and Trial Procedures
- Courtroom Demeanor and Testimony
- Legal Defense
- Burden of Proof
- Legal Terms and Definitions
- Court Structure
- Use of Force

Other areas that receive coverage in this section include such topics as the following:

- Constitutional Law Overview
- Evidence Concepts
- Evidence Rules
- Probable Cause
- Arrest Laws
- Search and Seizure Concepts
- Criminal Mischief
- Involuntary Admission Procedures/Substance Abuse Services
- Baker Act
- Obstruction of Justice
- Extortion
- Arson
- Assault/Battery
- Sexual Battery and Sex Crimes
- Homicide
- Theft/Dealing in Stolen Property
- Robbery

Questions

1. Which of the following terms stands for the principles of honor, morality, and conduct?
   a. professionalism
   b. stereotyping
   c. values
   d. ethics
   e. service

2. Which of the terms listed below refer to pride in self and career, respect for others, and commitment to skill development?
   a. militarism
   b. patriotism
   c. professionalism
   d. perfectionism
   e. autonomy

3. Ethical conduct in corrections is an important consideration because
   a. management decisions are frequently related to the number of complaints in an officer's file
   b. the decisions made by individual officers have no relationship to the image of the department as a whole
   c. the improper actions of any officer are viewed by the public as representative of all officers
   d. subtle changes in officer behaviors can rapidly alter public opinions of the department
   e. all of the above

4. Which of the following represents the best definition of the term "gratuity" as it is used by members of the criminal justice system?
   a. anything that one person gives to another with the intention of making the receiver reciprocate in kind
   b. the donation of items from one entity to another for use as a tax deduction
   c. an officer working off duty to increase earnings without declaring income on his or her taxes
   d. thankfulness
   e. anything of value that one person gives to another with the intention of benefiting the giver because of the receiver's position or authority

5. A corrections officer who intentionally violates a prisoner's civil rights would be exhibiting what kind of behavior?
   a. uncompromising
   b. unethical
   c. unconscionable
   d. unintentional
   e. exemplary

6. Discourteous conduct and divulging confidential information are examples of what type of behavior?
   a. officious
   b. subversive
   c. unbiased
   d. exemplary
   e. unethical

7. Officer Murphy has been assigned to a wing which has been the scene of repeated violence among inmates. Officer Murphy has had several discussions with inmate Davis concerning the problem of officer understaffing. One night while Officer Murphy is talking with inmate Davis, Davis gives Officer Murphy one of his compact disks (a CD) as a token of his appreciation and thanks Officer Murphy for his frank discussions and concern. What concept does this scenario demonstrate?
   a. promoting the idea that special considerations may be expected in return for small favors
   b. communicating with clients to improve performance
   c. fostering positive relations with inmates
   d. dealing with the community in a manner calculated to instill respect
   e. the value of community-based corrections efforts

8. Bribery falls into which of the following categories?
   a. felony
   b. misdemeanor
   c. infraction
   d. capitol felony
   e. either a or b above, depending on the amount offered

9. Evaluate the following statements:

1. A bribe involves unlawful compensation or reward for past, present, or future performance of a public servant

2. Bribery is always a felony.

3. In order to have the crime of "bribery," the offer to reward must be made to, or solicited by, a public servant.

a. all three statements are true
b. only statements 1 & 2 are true
c. only statements 1 & 3 are true
d. only statements 2 & 3 are true
e. all three statements are false

10. What do the initials CJSTC stand for in Florida?

a. Criminal Justice System and Training Commission
b. Complete Justice Standards and Training Commission
c. Criminal Justice Standards and Training Commission
d. Comprehensive Justice Standards and Training Commission
e. Criminal Justice Standards and Training Curriculum

11. Which of the following is a goal of CJSTC?

a. improve the delivery of quality training
b. ensure job-relatedness in employment standards
c. increase the professionalism of corrections officers
d. a & b only
e. all of the above are CJSTC goals

12. Which of the following is NOT a responsibility of CJSTC?

a. establish uniform minimum training standards
b. establish correctional officer training programs
c. accredit local correctional facilities
d. certify training academy instructors
e. administer the salary incentive program

13. What does the term decertification mean?

a. the governor and the cabinet can revoke a correctional officer's driver's license
b. a corrections officer may have his or her occupational license revoked
c. a person who has completed the basic recruit training curriculum has failed the certification examination
d. the agency has lost its accreditation status
e. the grand jury has recommended that an agency be forced to relinquish its insurance coverage

14. Which of the following are grounds for decertification?

a. having pled not guilty to a charge involving perjury
b. failure to maintain good moral character
c. residing outside the jurisdiction of one's employing agency
d. not being promoted to the next rank within five years of the last promotion
e. none of the above

15. The Florida CJSTC is part of what organization?

a. Florida Department of Law Enforcement
b. Florida Prison Wardens Association
c. Florida Sheriffs Association
d. Florida Corrections Executive Foundation
e. Florida Governor's Council

16. Evaluate the following three statements:

1. The Auburn Prison was built with the philosophy that fear of crime and silent confinement would result in crime prevention.

2. During medieval Europe, crime was considered to be an act that threatened the Church's authority.

3. Personal revenge was the typical reaction to crime and criminals in ancient times.

a. all three statements are true
b. only statements 1 & 2 are true
c. only statements 1 & 3 are true
d. only statements 2 & 3 are true
e. all three statements are false

17. Evaluate the following three statements:

1. Prisons are local facilities that hold prisoners prior to trial.

2. Jails house convicted felons who are serving long sentences.

3. Prisons house some nondangerous inmates who are serving short sentences for minor offenses.

a. all three statements are true
b. only statements 1 & 2 are true
c. only statements 1 & 3 are true
d. only statements 2 & 3 are true
e. all three statements are false

18. Which branch of Florida government is responsible for establishing and developing criminal law?
a. legislative
b. judicial
c. executive
d. all of the above
e. none of the above

19. Which of the following is NOT a part of the American criminal justice system?
a. mental health
b. law enforcement
c. courts
d. corrections
e. all are members

20. Which of the following parties is not a member of the court system?
a. state attorney
b. sheriff
c. judge
d. plaintiff's attorney
e. clerk of the court

21. Which of the following parties prosecutes all felony and misdemeanor criminal cases on behalf of the State of Florida?
a. clerk of the court
b. public defender's office
c. plaintiff's attorney
d. judge
e. state attorney

22. Which of the following parties records the testimony and proceedings, complete with objections, rulings, exceptions, as well as oral and written charges of the court, in any criminal case in circuit court?
a. state attorney
b. clerk of the court
c. public defender
d. plaintiff's attorney
e. court reporter

23. What is the name for a body of citizens sworn to deliver a true verdict upon evidence submitted to them in a trial?
a. grand jury
b. grand inquisitor
c. voir dire
d. coroner's inquest
e. trial jury

24. Which of the following parties is responsible for filing an "information" as a formal criminal charge?
a. state attorney
b. law enforcement officer
c. public defender
d. judge
e. jury foreman

25. Officer Jones has received an official piece of paper from the Sheriff's Office. This paper instructs Officer Jones to appear at the courthouse in the matter of the State of Florida vs. John Doe on March 10th at 8:30 AM for a deposition. Which of the following persons would one NOT expect to be present at the deposition?
a. a state attorney
b. a defense attorney
c. judge
d. stenographer
e. none of the above

26. A person who is found guilty of a misdemeanor and who receives a punishment of imprisonment will serve time in what type of a facility?
a. state penitentiary
b. federal institution
c. regional holding facility
d. county jail
e. none of the above

27. Which of the following is NOT a member of the Florida correctional system?
a. county jails
b. state penitentiaries
c. probation offices
d. grammar schools
e. work-release centers

28. Prisons typically fall under which level of government?
    a. city
    b. county
    c. state
    d. federal
    e. international

29. Which level of government typically oversees jails?
    a. city
    b. county
    c. state
    d. federal
    e. international

30. Which of the following terms refers to the hope that being punished or seeing somebody else punished will prevent future criminal behavior?
    a. incapacitation
    b. retribution
    c. deterrence
    d. rehabilitation
    e. none of the above

31. Which of the following terms implies that inmates, while in prison, undergo change so that when they are released they will be less likely to commit additional crimes?
    a. incapacitation
    b. retribution
    c. deterrence
    d. rehabilitation
    e. none of the above

32. Which of the following terms best explains why prisons have education, counseling, and vocational training programs for inmates?
    a. incapacitation
    b. retribution
    c. deterrence
    d. rehabilitation
    e. none of the above

33. Which of the following terms is associated with the word "revenge?"
    a. incapacitation
    b. retribution
    c. deterrence
    d. rehabilitation
    e. none of the above

34. The phrase "an eye for an eye, a tooth for a tooth" best fits which of the following terms?
    a. incapacitation
    b. retribution
    c. deterrence
    d. rehabilitation
    e. none of the above

35. Which of the following terms means that a person in confinement is not able to victimize law-abiding citizens in the free world?
    a. incapacitation
    b. retribution
    c. deterrence
    d. rehabilitation
    e. none of the above

36. Which of the following terms means that punishment should be severe enough to make people avoid that act in the future?
    a. incapacitation
    b. retribution
    c. deterrence
    d. rehabilitation
    e. none of the above

37. Evaluating the following statements:

    1. One responsibility of corrections is to provide inmates with opportunities to change and to encourage inmates to change.

    2. The county sheriff is the person who decides what the terms and conditions of a person's probation should be.

    3. Sheriff deputies are responsible for monitoring persons who are under community supervision.

    a. all three statements are true
    b. only statements 1 & 2 are false
    c. only statements 1 & 3 are false
    d. only statements 2 & 3 are false
    e. all three statements are false

38. Suppose that inmates are credited with one day of time served for every two days they are not written up for rule violations or disruptive behaviors. Which of the following terms best describes this practice?

a. gain time
b. probation
c. parole
d. community supervision
e. out-bound placement

39. Evaluate the following statements:

1. Parole refers to being under community supervision instead of being incarcerated.

2. Probation refers to being under community supervision after being incarcerated.

3. Being released under gain time means that the person is no longer under supervision.

a. all three statements are true
b. only statements 1 & 2 are false
c. only statements 1 & 3 are false
d. only statements 2 & 3 are false
e. all three statements are false

40. Which of the following has the responsibility for deciding who gets placed on parole, the length of parole, and actions that should be taken if the conditions of parole are violated?

a. Crimes Compensation Board
b. Florida Association of Sheriffs
c. Parole Commission
d. Probation Commission
e. the trial judge

41. Which of the following is NOT a right afforded to persons accused of a crime?

a. be informed of the charge
b. speedy trial
c. confront and cross-examine witnesses
d. private trial
e. legal representation

42. Which of the following is NOT a right afforded to inmates?

a. adequate law library
b. voting in state elections
c. freedom from excessive punishments
d. religious freedom
e. adequate medical care

43. Evaluate the following statements:

1. All prisoners have the right to unrestricted visitations.

2. Severe overcrowding in a prison facility could amount to a cruel and unusual punishment.

3. Inmate rights may be limited so as to ensure order within the institution or if there is a compelling state interest.

a. all three statements are false
b. only statements 1 & 2 are true
c. only statements 1 & 3 are true
d. only statements 2 & 3 are true
e. all three statements are true

44. To what does the term "privileged relationship" refer?

a. a friendship where one party is extremely happy to be acquainted with the other
b. a relationship that keeps one party from divulging what another party said to him or her in confidence
c. the inability to issue a trespass warning to a person who has the right to be present at a location
d. a "set-aside" that is earmarked for members of a particular group
e. the status that goes along with a member of a socially significant group

45. Which of the following is NOT a privileged relationship?

a. priest-penitent
b. boyfriend-girlfriend
c. lawyer-client
d. doctor-patient
e. husband-wife

46. Evaluate the following statements:

1. An inmate has the right to be present whenever a corrections officer opens any of the inmate's legal correspondence to inspect it for contraband.

2. An inmate can be moved to isolation without a hearing if the inmate poses an immediate danger to self, others, or property.

3. Corrections officer can conduct warrantless searches of inmate cells.

a. all three statements are true
b. only statements 1 & 2 are true
c. only statements 1 & 3 are true
d. only statements 2 & 3 are true
e. all three statements are false

47. Evaluate the following statements:

 1. A corrections officer may search a visitor prior to a contact visit with an electronic searching device only if the corrections officer has obtained a search warrant first.

 2. Pretrial detainees should be kept separate from sentenced inmates whenever possible.

 3. The "Corrrectional Officers' Bill of Rights" applies only in civil cases.

 a. all three statements are false
 b. only statements 1 & 2 are false
 c. only statements 1 & 3 are false
 d. only statements 2 & 3 are false
 e. all three statements are true

48. The "Correctional Officers' Bill of Rights" does NOT address which of the following?

 a. standards regarding questioning
 b. officer's right to have an attorney present
 c. retaliation against an officer who exercises his or her rights
 d. notice of disciplinary action
 e. the bill addresses all of these areas

49. The purpose of law is to:

 a. define the parameters of public and private property
 b. preserve order
 c. protect persons
 d. protect property
 e. all of the above

50. One goal of law is to:

 a. promote economic prosperity
 b. provide jobs
 c. establish public relations
 d. guarantee rights
 e. ensure toadyism

51. Which of the following codes is the FIRST known written legal document that represents the idea of natural law?

 a. Justinian Code
 b. Military Code of Conduct
 c. Code of Hammurabi
 d. Correctional Officer's Code of Ethics
 e. The Early Code

52. The laws that are in place in this country can be traced back to which of the following traditions?

 a. the Teutonic codes
 b. English custom or case law
 c. Italian City States
 d. Spanish Maritime Law
 e. Indian tribal customs

53. What kind of law are people referring to when they talk about principles which derive their authority solely from usage and custom?

 a. criminal
 b. civil
 c. case
 d. statutory
 e. common

54. What type of laws are more concerned with private rights and appropriate monetary remedies when those rights are not honored or are violated?

 a. civil
 b. natural
 c. criminal
 d. common
 e. statutory

55. Rules, regulations, orders, and decisions created by administrative agencies to guide their internal operations are known as which of the following?

 a. common law
 b. case law
 c. administrative law
 d. civil law
 e. statutory law

56. A violation of somebody's rights because of either that person's race or gender would be an example of what kind of law?

 a. case
 b. statutory
 c. administrative
 d. international
 e. civil

57. What is the appropriate term to use when one is talking about the aggregate of reported cases as forming a body of jurisprudence, or the law of a particular subject as formed by the adjudged cases?

a. criminal law
b. civil law
c. case law
d. common law
e. constitutional law

58. Evaluate the following statements:

1. All people stand as equals before the law and, therefore, have certain rights.

2. The purpose of government is to secure rights for its people.

3. Government is the agent of the people, not their master.

a. all three statements are true
b. only statements 1 & 2 are true
c. only statements 1 & 3 are true
d. only statements 2 & 3 are true
e. all three statements are false

59. Which of the following crimes is the only offense specifically mentioned in the Florida Constitution?

a. murder
b. burglary
c. treason
d. perjury
e. mayhem

60. What kind of laws typically contain such penalties as prison or jail time?

a. criminal
b. natural
c. civil
d. common
e. infractions

61. Which of the following is "an infraction punishable only by fine or other civil penalty?"

a. criminal traffic violation
b. noncriminal traffic violation
c. incident
d. city ordinance violation
e. juvenile delinquency

62. The maximum amount of imprisonment that may be imposed for a noncriminal violation is:

a. 10 days
b. 15 days
c. 30 days
d. 1 year
e. none of the above

63. A municipal or county ordinance may be:

a. administrative in nature
b. criminal in nature
c. civil in nature
d. both b & c

64. Which of the following is the maximum term of imprisonment in the county jail for a first degree misdemeanor?

a. 60 days
b. 90 days
c. 180 days
d. 365 days
e. 5 years

65. What is the maximum term of imprisonment in jail for a second degree misdemeanor in Florida?

a. 15 days
b. 30 days
c. 60 days
d. 90 days
e. 180 days

66. Which of the following is the maximum punishment for a third degree felony?

a. 1 year imprisonment and a $500 fine
b. 2 years imprisonment and a $1,000 fine
c. 5 years imprisonment and a $5,000 fine
d. 10 years imprisonment and a $10,000 fine
e. 25 years imprisonment and a $100,000 fine

67. Evaluate the following three statements:

1. Administrative and regulatory laws may impose noncriminal sanctions.

2. A noncriminal violation cannot result in a fine against the defendant.

3. A misdemeanor of the first degree is punishable by a term of imprisonment not to exceed one year.

a. all three statements are true
b. only statements 1 & 2 are true
c. only statements 1 & 3 are true
d. only statements 2 & 3 are true
e. all three statements are false

68. A capital felony in Florida is punishable by a term of imprisonment:

    a. not to exceed 15 years
    b. not to exceed 30 years
    c. for life, not less than 25 years
    d. there are no provisions for imprisonment since the death penalty is automatic
    e. that the judge thinks is appropriate

69. Evaluate the following three statements:

    1. An individual may be imprisoned in a state penitentiary for any term which exceeds six months.

    2. An offense is a felony if it is punishable by death or imprisonment in the state penitentiary.

    3. Felonies and misdemeanors are classified by degree to identify the seriousness of the crime.

    a. all three statements are true
    b. only statements 1 & 2 are true
    c. only statements 1 & 3 are true
    d. only statements 2 & 3 are true
    e. all three statements are false

70. What is the maximum term of imprisonment for a felony of the first degree in Florida?

    a. 10 years
    b. 20, or when specifically provided, for a term of years not to exceed life imprisonment
    c. 25 years, or when specifically provided, for a term of years not to exceed life imprisonment
    d. 30 years, or when specifically provided, for a term of years not to exceed life imprisonment
    e. 40 years

71. Research shows that a small number of offenders are responsible for a substantial and disproportionate number of serious crimes committed in Florida. Which of the following terms best describes this group?

    a. career criminals
    b. habitual offenders
    c. psychopaths
    d. juveniles
    e. recidivists

72. What are the two basic elements of criminal liability that the state must prove in order to obtain a conviction?

    a. the suspect received personal gain from the act and the act was illegal
    b. the suspect's motive and the victim's state of mind
    c. motive and opportunity
    d. a crime was committed intentionally and the person charged was the one who committed the crime
    e. all of the above

73. Evaluate the following statements:

    1. To prove that a crime has taken place, it is necessary to show that all the statutory elements were violated.

    2. "Mens rea" is defined as criminal intent.

    3. Usually the defense of intoxication is successful if the alcohol was self-induced.

    a. all three statements are true
    b. only statements 1 & 2 are true
    c. only statements 1 & 3 are true
    d. only statements 2 & 3 are true
    e. all three statements are false

74. The criminal justice term "mens rea" is best described by which of the following phrases?

    a. "a state of mind of the actor, or his intent"
    b. a state of mind bent on the commission of an offense
    c. a necessary material element of the crime
    d. all of the above
    e. none of the above

75. Which of the following persons is presumed NOT to possess a mens rea?

    a. a six-year-old child
    b. a normal adult
    c. a person who is under the influence of alcohol
    d. a person who is under the influence of cocaine
    e. a person who is under the influence of a medical prescription

76. What is the meaning of the legal term "intent"?

    a. unintentionally doing that which the law declares to be a crime
    b. unknowingly doing that which the law declares to be a crime
    c. lacks a mens rea
    d. the absence of actus rea
    e. doing on purpose that which the law declares to be a crime

77. Evaluate the following three statements:

1. A factor to be considered in determining whether a person can be convicted of being an accessory after the fact to a crime committed by a second person is the relationship by blood or marriage between the two persons.

2. A person can be convicted of a crime as a principal to the crime if he or she did not actually do anything to help commit the crime, but only knew what was going to happen and did nothing to stop it.

3. A wife can be convicted of accessory after the fact to murder if she helps her husband dispose of the murder weapon knowing that he committed murder with it.

a. all three statements are false
b. only statements 1 & 2 are false
c. only statements 1 & 3 are false
d. only statements 2 & 3 are false
e. all three statements are true

78. Julio and Mike are inmates in a Florida prison. Julio tells Mike that he has just stabbed Adam, another inmate. Mike takes Julio's knife and hides it under his mattress so the corrections officers cannot find it. What role has Mike played in this event?

a. accessory before the fact
b. accessory after the fact
c. principal in the first degree
d. habitual offender
e. chronic offender

79. Ray's wife, Martha, refuses to grant him a divorce. In desperation, Ray contacts Harold who is a professional killer. Harold agrees to kill Martha and make it look like an accident for the price of $10,000 in cash. Which of the following terms best describes this situation?

a. conspiracy to commit homicide
b. dereliction of duty
c. reasonable suspicion
d. solicitation to commit homicide
e. attempted homicide

80. Ray's wife, Martha, refuses to grant him a divorce. In desperation, Ray contacts Cynthia whom he thinks is a professional killer but is really an undercover police officer. Cynthia pretends to agree to kill Martha and make it look like an accident for the price of $10,000 in cash. Which of the following terms best describes this situation?

a. attempted homicide
b. conspiracy to commit homicide
c. solicitation to commit homicide
d. dereliction of duty
e. reasonable suspicion

81. In general, what is the punishment for any attempt, conspiracy, or solicitation to commit a crime?

a. the same as the actual commission
b. one degree higher than the actual commission
c. two degrees lower than the actual commission
d. one degree lower than the actual commission
e. there is no difference

82. Evaluate the following statements:

1. To be a "principal" in the first degree, the defendant does not have to be present when the crime is committed or attempted.

2. Accessory after the fact is considered a felony according to Florida law.

3. Solicitation is a civil infraction.

a. all three statements are true
b. only statements 1 & 2 are true
c. only statements 1 & 3 are true
d. only statements 2 & 3 are true
e. all three statements are false

83. Which of the following actions would fall under an intentional tort?

a. failure to train
b. inadequate supervision
c. excessive use of force
d. rudeness
e. decertificaton

84. Which of the following actions would fall under an negligence tort?

a. failure to train
b. false imprisonment
c. excessive use of force
d. rudeness
e. emotional distress

85. A civil wrong in which the action or inaction of one person causes injury or harm to another in violation of a legal duty imposed by law is called what?

a. civil liability
b. duces tecum
c. a tort
d. voir dire
e. functional imperative

86. What is criminal liability?

a. responsibility for acts of good faith
b. responsibility for a violation of state or federal criminal laws
c. responsibility for compensatory damages
d. responsibility for punitive damages
e. the same thing as civil liability

87. Which of the following is a necessary element when trying to prove liability?

a. reasonable concern
b. done in good faith
c. wrongful act
d. done in accordance with state statute
e. none of the above

88. When a person is judged to be civilly liable for lost wages and medical bills, for what type of damages is he or she responsible?

a. compensatory damages
b. aggravated damages
c. mitigating damages
d. punitive damages
e. conciliatory damages

89. When a person is judged to be civilly liable for pain and suffering, for what type of damages is he or she responsible?

a. compensatory damages
b. aggravated damages
c. intentional damages
d. punitive damages
e. conciliatory damages

90. What kind of penalty may the court assess in a civil action so as to discourage or deter further misconduct?

a. punitive damages
b. court costs
c. compensatory damages
d. actual damages
e. a fine

91. Monetary damage awards which will barely compensate the plaintiff for his or her actual loss are referred to as which of the following?

a. punitive damage
b. personal damages
c. liability damages
d. compensatory damages
e. conciliatory damages

92. What type of liability does a supervisor incur for the conduct or actions of employees under his or her authority and responsibility?

a. general liability
b. vicarious liability
c. administrative liability
d. specific liability
e. none of the above

93. The term "vicarious liability" refers to which of the following?

a. credibility given to an eyewitness of a correctional officer's misconduct
b. expert witness testimony under oath
c. supervisory responsibility
d. criminal intent
e. the formula that the judge uses to arrive at a settlement figure for damages

94. What is another meaning for the legal term "vicarious liability?"

a. excessive force
b. excessive use of weapon
c. intentional tort
d. indirect responsibility
e. direct responsibility

95. Corrections officers can incur civil liabilities in a number of different ways. Which of the following areas is NOT one of those ways?

a. improper search and seizure
b. negligent vehicle operation
c. excessive use of force
d. interfering with an inmate's right to access legal counsel
e. corrections officers can incur civil liability in all of the above areas

96. Which of the following is NOT an element of a tort?

a. duty
b. breach of duty
c. harm done
d. prima facie damages
e. proximate or direct cause

97. Which of the following actions does NOT prevent or protect against a lawsuit?

a. knowledge of the law
b. documentation
c. policy and procedures within constitutional guidelines
d. aggressive and up-to-date departmental training program
e. increased departmental budget

98. What are the elements of a deprivation of rights in a federal lawsuit brought under a Section 1983 action?

a. any public official or administrator
b. who violates a person's Constitutional rights
c. under color of law
d. all of the above
e. a & b above only

99. Which of the following is NOT a valid defense for a corrections officer charged with a civil violation?

a. done in good faith
b. during an unlawful use of a weapon
c. adhered to departmental policy
d. according to prior training
e. injured party contributed to his or her own injuries

100. A lawsuit involving a federal civil rights violation is also known as what?

a. Section 1983 action
b. Section 2002 action
c. mediation
d binding arbitration
e. legislative redress

101. An officer who uses excessive force in the performance of his or her duties could be charged with violating which of the following?

a. federal law (8th Amendment)
b. state law (battery)
c. departmental policy and procedures
d. civil law
e. all of the above

102. The court finds a corrections officer guilty of committing an intentional act that caused a monetary loss to the victim. What is the term for the monetary damages awarded to that victim?

a. actual damages
b. compensatory damages
c. negligent damages
d. punitive damages
e. conciliatory damages

103. A court finds a corrections officer guilty of an intentional unlawful act which resulted in the physical injury of an innocent bystander. What is the term for damages awarded in an attempt to discourage similar behavior?

a. actual damages
b. compensatory damages
c. punitive damages
d. vicarious damages
e. conciliatory damages

104. A corrections officer is most likely to incur civil liability through which of the following acts while performing his or her duties?

a. done in accordance with departmental policy
b. done in good faith
c. done unlawfully
d. justified under the law
e. none of the above

105. Evaluate the following three statements:

1. In Florida, a corrections officer may use "good faith" as a defense against a civil action.

2. In an action under Section 1983 of Title 42, U.S. Code, the behavior complained of must have deprived the plaintiff of rights, privileges, or immunities secured by the U.S. Constitution.

3. The doctrine of vicarious liability protects correctional executives from being sued in a civil lawsuit when a subordinate officer commits a civil rights violation.

a. all three statements are true
b. only statements 1 & 2 are true
c. only statements 1 & 3 are true
d. only statements 2 & 3 are true
e. all three statements are false

106. Evaluate the following three statements:

1. Punitive damages awards are usually awarded against the defendant as means of punishment.

2. Public service officials cannot be charged civilly and criminally due to double jeopardy (5th Amendment).

3. A wrongful act, failure to properly act, negligent or reckless act by an officer may result in monetary damage awards against the officer and/or agency.

a. all three statements are true
b. only statements 1 & 2 are true
c. only statements 1 & 3 are true
d. only statements 2 & 3 are true
e. all three statements are false

107. Evaluate the following statements:

1. Perjury is defined as making a false statement, not believed to be true, under oath in an official or unofficial proceeding.

2. Administrative and regulatory law may impose noncriminal sanctions such as fines, license revocation or suspension, and restitution.

3. A corrections officer who pleads guilty or is found guilty of perjury may be subject to decertification.

a. all three statements are true
b. only statements 1 & 2 are true
c. only statements 1 & 3 are true
d. only statements 2 & 3 are true
e. all three statements are false

108. Which of the following best describes the statement "corruptly to give, offer, or promise to any public servant, or, if a public servant, corruptly to request, solicit, accept or agree to accept any pecuniary or other benefit with an intent to influence the performance of any act or omission which the person believes to be, or the public servant represents as being, within the official discretion of a public servant, in violation of a public duty, or in performance of a public duty?"

a. perjury
b. negligence
c. bribery
d. gambling
e. recantation

109. Inmate Watson hands Officer Andrews a letter, along with a $20 bill, and asks Officer Andrews if he would skip the correctional institute's mail facility and instead drop the letter off at the post office in town while Officer Andrews is on his way home. Which of the following best describes this event?

a. perjury
b. negligence
c. bribery
d. gambling
e. recantation

110. Officer Jones has received an official piece of paper from the Sheriff's Office. This paper instructs her to appear at the courthouse in the matter of the State of Florida vs. John Doe on March 10th at 8:30 AM for a deposition. Which of the following terms bests describes this paper?

a. indictment
b. information
c. subpoena
d. writ of habeaus corpus
e. decree

111. Officer Smith has received an official piece of paper from the Sheriff's Office. This paper instructs Officer Smith to appear in felony court in the matter of the State of Florida vs. John Doe on March 1 at 8:30 AM for a trial proceeding. Which of the following terms best describes that piece of paper?

a. injunction
b. capias
c. subpoena
d. summons
e. affidavit

112. Officer Collins is subpoenaed to appear in a criminal trial as a witness against an inmate who stabbed another inmate. As the proceedings begin, the defense attorney advises the judge that he wishes to invoke the "Rule." How does this action affect Officer Collins?

a. Officer Collins can discuss the case with anybody, such as a newspaper reporter, outside of the courtroom
b. it has no effect on Officer Collins because the "Rule" pertains only to lawyer conduct
c. it has no effect on Officer Collins because the "Rule" pertains only to the judge
d. Officer Collins may not discuss the case with anybody outside of the courtroom, except for the lawyers involved in the case
e. it has no effect on Officer Collins because the "Rule" pertains only to the jury

113. Who can issue a subpoena?

a. the judge
b. the state attorney or a defense attorney
c. the sheriff
d. clerk of court
e. the supervisor of elections

114. What does the legal term "duces tecum" mean when included in a subpoena?

a. bring the defendant
b. bring the deposition
c. bring the witness
d. bring the victim
e. bring the records

115. Evaluate the following three statements:

1. An officer who fails to comply with the requirements of a subpoena may be reprimanded by his or her department or the judge of a given court but does not risk civil or criminal contempt proceedings.

2. In order to obtain a conviction for a crime, the state must prove that a majority of elements for that crime exists.

3. Once the state has proven that a crime was committed it also has to prove that the defendant is the one who committed the crime in order to obtain a conviction.

a. all three statements are false
b. only statements 1 & 2 are false
c. only statements 1 & 3 are false
d. only statements 2 & 3 are false
e. all three statements are true

116. The State of Florida requires that a person who has been arrested and placed in jail must be afforded first appearance within how many hours?

a. 12
b. 24
c. 32
d. 72
e. 96

117. Which of the following items will the judge be most interested in reviewing at first appearance?

a. the officer's arrest procedure
b. the officer's offense report
c. the officer's criminal history check of the defendant
d. the officer's probable cause affidavit
e. the officer's adherence to agency policy guidelines

118. A person who has been arrested but does not make bail must be given a "Preliminary Hearing" within how many days?

a. 1 day
b. 3 days
c. 10 days
d. 30 days
e. 60 days

119. Which of the following characterizes a deposition hearing?

a. is generally called by the defense attorney
b. testimony will be sworn and recorded
c. requires that the officer answer questions asked by the defense attorney
d. all of the above
e. a & b above only

120. Which of the following is NOT an appropriate plea in a criminal case?

a. not guilty
b. not guilty by reason of insanity
c. nolo contendere
d. guilty
e. innocent

121. Once a jury is seated in a criminal case, the next step consists of what?

a. the judge gives sentencing instructions to the jury
b. the state rests its case
c. the defense presents its evidence and testimony
d. the judge orders a presentence investigation be conducted
e. a statement of the charges against the defendant is read to the jury

122. At what point must a defendant must be afforded the opportunity to obtain advice from an attorney?

a. prior to first appearance
b. prior to arraignment
c. prior to sentencing
d. prior to arrest
e. prior to trial

123. Sometimes a defendant does not plead "guilty" or "not guilty" to the charges in a criminal case. Instead, the defendant indicates that he or she will not contest the penalty that the court imposes. Which of the following terms refers to this practice?

a. nolo contendere
b. corpus delicti
c. nolle prosequi
d. modus operandi
e. assumption of innocence

124. Which side presents its evidence and testimony first in a criminal prosecution?

a. the judge
b. the state
c. the defendant
d. the order is determined at random
e. the jury

125. Under what conditions can a judge declare a mistrial?

a. if the jury cannot reach a unanimous verdict
b. if the judge determines that some event has occurred that interferes with the jury's ability to remain impartial and objective
c. the defendant is found guilty
d. all of the above
e. only a & b above

126. What phase of a criminal justice proceeding is concerned with determining a proper penalty for the defendant?

a. sentencing
b. voir dire
c. deposition
d. arraignment
e. first appearance

127. Evaluate the following three statements:

1. A criminal defendant in a jury trial can be found guilty by a majority of votes from jurors.

2. The purpose of cross-examination is to impeach the credibility of the witness.

3. An "arraignment" occurs after the filing of formal charges.

a. all three statements are true
b. only statements 1 & 2 are true
c. only statements 1 & 3 are true
d. only statements 2 & 3 are true
e. all three statements are false

128. Evaluate the following three statements with respect to officer involvement in court proceedings:

1. An officer may use notes taken during his or her investigation to refresh his or her memory.

2. An officer testifying as a witness should not restrict his or her answers to questions from attorneys to the question asked, but should be sure to add information he or she feels is pertinent to the case.

3. An officer who is waiting in the witness room with other witnesses prior to testifying should interrogate defense witnesses in order to find out what they are going to say and pass that information along to the assistant state attorney prosecuting the case.

a. all three statements are true
b. only statements 1 & 2 are false
c. only statements 1 & 3 are false
d. only statements 2 & 3 are false
e. all three statements are false

129. When a corrections officer is called to the stand as a witness, his or her testimony to the jury should be what?

a. neutral and objective
b. factual

c. slanted towards the state attorney handling the case
d. all of the above
e. a & b above only

130. When testifying on the witness stand, the officer should direct his or her courtroom testimony to which of the following parties?

a. the court reporter
b. the bailiff
c. the audience
d. the attorney asking the question
e. the trial jury

131. Which of the following actions would be inappropriate behavior for an officer to display when giving testimony under oath?

a. being courteous
b. avoiding bias and prejudice
c. guessing at the question if he or she does not know the answer
d. being concise and expressive
e. avoiding a monotone voice when speaking

132. What is the courtroom tactic called when a lawyer lulls the witness into a false sense of security to get answers that favor his or her side of the case?

a. rapid-fire questioning
b. badgering the witness
c. friendly counsel
d. being belligerent to the witness
e. condescending counsel

133. What does it mean when the trial judge sustains one attorney's objection to the other attorney's question?

a. the witness has to answer the question
b. the witness does not have to answer the question
c. the jury must leave the courtroom
d. the bailiff must leave the courtroom
e. none of the above

134. Which of the following is NOT a reason for an objection to be raised by an opposing attorney?

a. leading questions on direct examination
b. questioning within the proper scope
c. irrelevancy
d. calling for the conclusion of a witness

135. When an officer is testifying in court and the defense attorney demands that the officer give either a "yes" or a "no" response, the officer:

a. has no choice except to answer either "yes" or "no"
b. may refuse to answer the question by advising the defense he refuses to do so
c. may ask the state's attorney if he can answer the questions with qualifications
d. refuse to answer by invoking the 5th Amendment privilege
e. may ask the judge if he can answer the questions with qualifications

136. Evaluate the following three statements:

1. A "mistrial" may be declared in a criminal case if the jury cannot reach a unanimous verdict.

2. Depositions cannot be used to destroy the credibility of a witness.

3. Field notes may not be used for reference when testifying at a trial.

a. all three statements are false
b. only statements 1 & 2 are false
c. only statements 1 & 3 are false
d. only statements 2 & 3 are false
e. all three statements are true

137. Evaluate the following three statements:

1. When giving testimony, you should always display a sincere interest in the truth and accuracy of your statement.

2. Rapid-fire questioning is a tactic used by opposing counsel to attempt to force inconsistent answers from the witness.

3. Testimony given during a deposition is considered to be unsworn.

a. all three statements are true
b. only statements 1 & 2 are true
c. only statements 1 & 3 are true
d. only statements 2 & 3 are true
e. all three statements are false

138. Suppose that inmates Bill and Clyde tell Ed that an accomplice in the outside world has kidnapped Dawn who is Ed's daughter. Bill and

Clyde tell Ed that if he does not help them in their escape plans, they will kill Dawn. Furthermore, Bill and Clyde tell Ed that if he does help them escape, they will release Dawn unharmed. Ed participates in the escape effort, but is captured by correctional oficers. If you were Ed's defense attorney, which of the following legal defenses would you use in court to gain an acquittal for Ed?

a. immunity
b. entrapment
c. duress
d. self-defense
e. statute of limitations

139. John walks into the warden's office and tells the warden that his conscience is bothering him for a crime he committed and now he has decided to make a confession. John tells the warden that 15 years ago he stole three cans of paint from the local Sears store. If you were John's public defender, which of the following legal defenses would you use in court to gain an acquittal for John?

a. immunity
b. duress
c. entrapment
d. statute of limitations
e. self-defense

140. Which of the following defenses could a defendant raise at his or her trial?

a. coercion, statute of limitations, entrapment, self-defense
b. insanity, alibi, consent, conspiracy
c. entrapment, alibi, self-defense, solicitation
d. consent, alibi, self-defense, conspiracy
e. all of the above

141. What is the degree of proof that the state must achieve in order to obtain a criminal conviction?

a. a preponderance of the evidence
b. proof beyond a reasonable doubt
c. proof beyond all doubt
d. probable cause
e. reasonable suspicion

142. What is the degree of proof that the court uses in a civil case?

a. a preponderance of the evidence
b. proof beyond a reasonable doubt
c. proof beyond all doubt
d. a reasonable conclusion
e. reasonable suspicion

143. What is the criminal justice term for taking a person into custody so that he or she may be held to answer for a crime?

a. corpus delicti
b. arrest
c. habeas corpus
d. indictment
e. citation

144. Which of the following phrases gives the best definition of the legal term "confiscate?"

a. deed away some right or property
b. retain, care for, or keep someone or something for violation of a law
c. take and carry away property belonging to another
d. take or appropriate property seized for a violation of law
e. none of the above

145. Which of the following best defines what the word "crime" means?

a. city or county ordinance violation
b. regulatory violation
c. administrative rule violation
d. felony or misdemeanor
e. a breach of etiquette

146. Which of the following terms refers to a sworn written statement that provides the basis for an arrest warrant?

a. deposition
b. indictment
c. information
d. affidavit
e. res gestae

147. What is the criminal justice term that refers to a person admitting that he or she is the one who committed a particular crime?

a. contribution
b. testimony
c. confession

d. recanting
e. explanation

148. Legally depriving a person of liberty or freedom to move about as he or she chooses, or taking a person into custody to be held to answer for a crime is best described by which of the following terms?

a. arraignment
b. admission of guilt
c. arrest
d. mens rea
e. mala in se

149. The proof that a crime has been committed is known as:

a. evidence
b. stare decisis
c. data
d. modus operandi
e. mens rea

150. The word "defendant" refers to

a. the arresting officer
b. assistant state attorney handling the case
c. the party charged with a crime
d. public defender handling the case
e. the courtroom in which the case is being handled

151. When the criminal court judge sentences the defendant to pay a specific amount of money to the victim for damages or losses the defendant caused, what is the judge ordering?

a. damages
b. forfeiture
c. seizure
d. restitution
e. compensation

152. Florida Statute 776.06 defines "deadly force" as that level of force likely to cause what type of an outcome?

a. a felony charge to be filed
b. a formal criminal charge to be filed
c. an indictment by a grand jury
d. an internal affairs investigation
e. a death or great bodily harm

153. The Baker Act sets forth the procedures for legally handling which types of individuals?

a. mentally ill
b. alcoholics
c. child abuse victims
d. physically handicapped
e. workers who are injured while on the job

154. The "Treatment and Rehabilitation of Drug Dependents Act" sets forth the procedures for legally handling which of the following types of individuals?

a. mentally ill
b. alcoholics
c. child abuse victims
d. physically handicapped
e. workers who are injured while on the job

155. The legal term "indictment" refers to a criminal charge that is issued by which of the following parties?

a. state attorney
b. judge
c. trial jury
d. sheriff
e. grand jury

156. What does the criminal justice term "information" mean?

a. a formal charge issued by a grand jury
b. a criminal's method of operation
c. a person who provides intelligence concerning law violators
d. a formal criminal charge filed by the state attorney
e. any intelligence reports that the police create

157. Which of the following phrases best describes the legal term "modus operandi?"

a. mandated operations
b. method of operation
c. method of orientation
d. modern operations
e. model opinion

158. Which phrase most accurately describes what takes place at an arraignment?

a. probable cause hearing
b. a "True Bill" is returned

c. motion to suppress
d. interrogation
e. the accused enters a plea

159. Which of the following terms refers to money that a defendant surrenders in order to remain out of jail and to ensure that he or she will appear at a later date in court to answer charges?

a. bail
b. affirmation
c. pledge
d. waiver
e. bounty

160. Which of the following best describes what a deposition is?

a. sworn, recorded testimony given by a principal or a witness in a case during the trial
b. conversation between the trial judge and the jury
c. statements made at a sidebar
d. discussion held by the judge in chambers with the state attorney and the defendant's lawyer
e. sworn, recorded testimony given by a principal or a witness in a case prior to the trial

161. Which of the following terms refers to where the crime was committed and where the trial is being held?

a. voir dire
b. venue
c. corpus delicti
d. modus operandi
e. writ

162. Which of the following statements best describes bail and bond practices?

a. is money needed for release until trial
b. can be borrowed from bail bondsmen, usually at 10% premium
c. is returned at the close of the case
d. all of the above are true
e. b & c only are true

163. Which of the following best describes the word "venue?"

a. the thing you look at in a restaurant before you order your meal
b. the circuit or county in which a particular trial may be held
c. a place where a law enforcement officer can store his or her equipment while inside the jail processing a prisoner
d. a piece of paper which demands that you be in court
e. a judge's sentencing instructions to the jury

164. Which of the following statements is the best example of what the term "nolo contendere" means?

a. the defendant pleads guilty because he or she does not have an alibi
b. the defendant does have a good alibi and, therefore, pleads not guilty
c. the defendant is going to fight the charges against him or her
d. the defendant elects not to contest the charges
e. the defendant does not wish to have an attorney represent him or her

165. When an officer takes possession of property because it is evidence or contraband, what lawful act is he or she performing?

a. a forfeiture
b. a search
c. an arrest
d. an abandonment
e. a seizure

166. An affidavit is a sworn written statement which could include:

a. a witness statement
b. a victim statement
c. information pertaining to an arrest
d. all of the above
e. none of the above

167. Due process of law involves the protection of such individual rights as:

a. right to public trial
b. right to effective counsel
c. notice of charges
d. all of the above

168. Which of the following terms refers to a formal criminal charge that is issued by a grand jury?

a. information
b. indictment

c. informant
d. arraignment
e. affidavit

169. Which of the following terms refers to goods, property or other things a person cannot legally have in his or her custody?

a. evidence
b. contraband
c. criminal byproduct
d. instrumentality
e. commodity

170. To what does the criminal justice term "actus reus" refer?

a. the criminal act or wrongful act
b. criminal intent
c. witnessing a crime in progress
d. reporting a crime to the police
e. not reporting a crime to the police

171. What is another term for jury selection?

a. venue
b. mens reus
c. voir dire
d. nolle prosequi
e. nolo contendere

172. The initials FCIC refer to which of the following?

a. Florida Center for International Counterintelligence
b. Florida Crime Information Center
c. Florida Criminal Information Center
d. Federal Crime Information Center
e. Federal Criminal Information and Counterintelligence

173. To what does the phrase "the legal capacity to distinguish right from wrong" refer?

a. one's character
b. reasonable suspicion
c. actus reus
d. mens rea
e. probable cause

174. What legal concept is conveyed by the following statement: "the circumstances are such that a reasonable person would conclude that the accused person is the one who committed the crime."

a. probable cause
b. reasonable suspicion
c. facsimile of justice
d. corpus delicti
e. ex post facto

175. During a legal proceeding the defendant's attorney makes a motion asking the judge to suppress his or her client's confession because of a Miranda violation. What exactly is the attorney asking the judge to do?

a. to award civil damages for a constitutional violation
b. to rule on whether the client actually confessed to the crime
c. to have the jury vote on whether or not to admit the confession
d. to allow the client to change his or her plea
e. to throw out the confession from further consideration

176. Which of the following parties can issue a search warrant?

a. state attorney
b. plaintiff's attorney
c. sheriff
d. clerk of the court
e. judge

177. Which of the following terms refers to the situation where a defendant's lawyer goes to a higher court to correct or modify a judgment or ruling in a lower court?

a. bail
b. appeal
c. writ of habeaus corpus
d. settlement
e. objection

178. Which of the following terms best describes the situation in which a convicted offender is not confined to a correctional facility but has his or her freedom restricted within the community or home and specific sanctions are imposed and enforced?

a. detention
b. visitation

c. community control
d. imprisonment
e. institutionalization

179. Which of the following terms best describes the situation in which a convicted offender is not confined to a correctional facility, lives within the community, but is required to make periodic contact with a community control officer?

a. detention
b. probation
c. community control
d. imprisonment
e. institutionalization

180. Which of the following terms is paired with the term "Miranda rights?"

a. interview
b. contraband
c. testimony
d. interrogation
e. statement

181. What concept is being referred to when positions within an organization are viewed in terms of levels or their relative authority to other positions?

a. chain of command
b. ladder of authority
c. obligatory duty
d. evidence preservation
e. line functions

182. How many levels of courts are there within the Florida judiciary?

a. 1
b. 2
c. 3
d. 4
e. 5

183. Which of the following types of cases come before county courts in Florida?

a. traffic infractions
b. misdemeanor cases
c. felony cases
d. all of the above
e. only a & b above

184. Suppose that Mr. Smith has decided to sue Mr. Jones for civil damages in the amount of five hundred dollars. In which court should Mr. Smith file the suit?

a. circuit court
b. county court
c. district court of appeals
d. The Florida Supreme Court
e. either a or c above

185. Mr. Perez was arrested by a Florida County Sheriff's Department on charges of first degree murder, a capital felony. A grand jury has indicted Mr. Perez and now the case goes to trial. In which of the following courts will the case be tried?

a. county court
b. district court of appeal
c. circuit court
d. Florida Supreme Court
e. civil court

186. A person who is charged with a "capital felony" will be tried in which court?

a. county court
b. district court of appeal
c. Florida Supreme Court
d. circuit court
e. any of the above depending on the judges' availability and calendars

187. If a person is charged with a capital crime, then he or she:

a. must be indicted by a grand jury
b. will have a 12-member jury at trial
c. could be punished by life in prison or death if convicted
d. all of the above
e. a & c above only

188. To what jurisdiction does a municipal ordinance typically apply?

a. a neighborhood
b. city
c. county
d. state
e. region

189. To which court is a juvenile referred after being arrested in a delinquency case?

a. county court
b. circuit court
c. district court of appeals
d. civil court
e. none of the above

190. To which part of the court system does traffic court belong?

a. county court
b. circuit court
c. district court of appeal
d. Florida Supreme Court
e. civil court

191. In which court are adult misdemeanor cases tried?

a. the supreme court
b. circuit court
c. county court
d. district court of appeals
e. civil court

192. Which of the following courts is responsible for disciplining attorneys?

a. county court
b. circuit court
c. district court of appeal
d. Florida Supreme Court
e. either county or circuit court, depending on the attorney's infraction

193. Officer Paschal is trying to arrest an unarmed suspect for a first-degree felony when the suspect physically attacks the officer. What type of force is Officer Paschal justified in using to prevent the suspect's escape and to protect himself from injury?

a. aggressive
b. aggravating
c. injuring
d. deadly
e. reasonable

194. Officer Paschal is trying to arrest a homicide suspect who is armed with a crowbar when the suspect physically attacks the officer. What type of force is Officer Paschal justified in using to protect himself from injury and to prevent the suspect's escape?

a. aggressive
b. aggravating
c. injuring
d. deadly
e. unreasonable

195. Officer Paschal is trying to arrest an unarmed suspect for a first degree misdemeanor when the suspect pushes the officer away. What type of force is Officer Paschal justified in using to prevent the suspect's escape and to protect himself from injury?

a. aggressive
b. aggravating
c. injuring
d. reasonable
e. deadly

196. Officer Paschal is trying to arrest an armed suspect for a traffic infraction when the suspect physically attacks the officer. What type of force is Officer Paschal justified in using to prevent the suspect's escape and to protect himself from injury?

a. aggressive
b. aggravating
c. injuring
d. outstanding
e. deadly

197. Officer Ames is going to arrest a suspect for a misdemeanor theft. The suspect cooperates fully with the officer's commands and does not offer any verbal nor physical resistance. What type of force should Officer Ames use to effect the arrest?

a. aggressive
b. controlling
c. injuring
d. aggravating
e. deadly

198. Which of the following should NOT be a factor when determining the need to use deadly force?

a. immediacy of the threat
b. suspect gender
c. threatening weapon's capabilities
d. threat to the lives of others

199. What term is defined as "the force an officer realistically believes to be necessary to defend himself or herself or another from bodily harm while making an arrest?"

a. controlling
b. deadly
c. injuring
d. reasonable
e. aggressive

200. What type of force is likely to cause great bodily harm?

a. deadly
b. aggravated
c. controlling
d. injuring
e. aggressive

201. What type of force is designed to subdue a subject without injury?

a. persuasive
b. controlling
c. physical
d. reasonable
e. aggressive

202. What would a positive aspect of the proper use of force include?

a. self-confidence
b. being aggressive
c. eliminating the need for backup
d. eliminating the officer's fear
e. none of the above

203. Evaluate the following three statements:

1. A corrections officer must consider whether there is an immediate threat of death or great personal injury when using deadly force.

2. Warning shots are to be used only when deadly force is not justified in an arrest.

3. The purpose of the use of force is the protection of persons and property, to enforce the law, and to maintain order and control of law violators.

a. all three statements are true
b. only statements 1 & 2 are true
c. only statements 1 & 3 are true
d. only statements 2 & 3 are true
e. all three statements are false

204. Evaluate the following statements:

1. Corrections officers are never permitted to use force to protect another person unless that person is another corrections officer.

2. Reasonable force is that level which is likely to cause death or great bodily harm.

3. Excessive force is defined as any force which the officer truly believes to be necessary to defend himself or another from bodily harm while making the arrest.

a. all three statements are true
b. only statements 1 & 2 are true
c. only statements 1 & 3 are true
d. only statements 2 & 3 are true
e. all three statements are false

205. Who has the responsibility to provide clear evidence to prove that the level of force that the officer employed was necessary and reasonable considering all circumstances?

a. the person against whom the force was directed
b. the agency's manager
c. any witness to the event
d. the officer using force
e. the officer's immediate supervisor

206. What type of payments may the court order if a corrections officer is found guilty of using excessive force in a grossly negligent or reckless manner?

a. attorney fees for the plaintiff
b. compensatory damages
c. punitive damages
d. a civil fine
e. all of the above

207. What kinds of information should a corrections officer include in a use of force report?

a. reasons for why he or she used force
b. physical and verbal resistance exhibited by suspect
c. specific force used by the officer
d. medical report detailing any injuries sustained by the suspect or by the officer
e. all of the above

208. Which of the following items when used properly constitute deadly force?

a. shotgun
b. OC spray
c. restraining devices
d. baton
e. stun gun

209. In general, with what type of issues is the United States Supreme Court concerned?

a. questions involving the federal Constitution
b. international disputes that the United Nations is unable to resolve
c. the application of pronouncements issued by the World Court to United States citizens
d. declarations of war issued by Congress
e. confirmation of Presidential nominees for high level posts

210. Which Amendment to the United States Constitution addresses freedom of speech?

a. 1st
b. 2nd
c. 4th
d. 5th
e. 14th

211. Which Amendment to the United States Constitution deals with the right of citizens to be secure from unreasonable searches and seizures?

a. 1st
b. 2nd
c. 4th
d. 5th
e. 14th

212. Which Amendment to the United States Constitution concerns protection from cruel and unusual punishments?

a. 1st
b. 2nd
c. 4th
d. 8th
e. 14th

213. Which of the following terms does NOT belong in this list?

a. evidence
b. contraband
c. mens rea
d. fruits of a crime
e. instrumentality

214. When a witness responds to questions while under oath and on the witness stand, he or she is providing what kind of evidence?

a. physical
b. documentary
c. testimonial
d. physical
e. circumstantial

215. The check which was passed in a forgery and uttering case would be an example of what kind of evidence?

a. circumstantial
b. testimonial
c. temporary
d. documentary
e. physical

216. What is the "exclusionary rule?"

a. evidence seized illegally cannot be used in court by the defense
b. testimony obtained during the course of a privileged relationship cannot be used in court
c. evidence seized illegally cannot be used in court by the prosecution
d. testimony from a co-defendant cannot be used in court by the prosecution if the co-defendant has agreed to testify in return for a reduced sentence
e. co-defendants can demand separate trials

217. What does the term "chain of custody" mean?

a. handcuffing procedures
b. a list of all persons who have handled a piece of evidence
c. a suspect who is arrested must be delivered to the jail for processing prior to any bond or bail consideration
d. a list of arresting officers
e. when the judge transfers a convicted suspect into the custody of the Department of Corrections after pronouncing the sentence

218. Ricky is on the witness stand and, in response to a question from the state attorney, testifies as to what Dawn told him about what Charles said. The defense attorney immediately objects to this line of questioning. On what basis is the defense attorney objecting?

a. privileged relationship
b. hearsay evidence
c. speculation
d. unwarranted conclusion
e. witness is not qualified as an expert in the area

219. Which of the following must be present in order for an officer to make a lawful arrest?

a. reasonable suspicion
b. petit suspicion
c. grand suspicion
d. probable suspicion
e. probable cause

220. The statement "facts which would lead a reasonably prudent officer, based upon his or her training and experience, to believe that a crime has been committed or is being committed" describes which of the following terms?

a. petit suspicion
b. reasonable suspicion
c. probable cause
d. grand suspicion
e. probable suspicion

221. Assume that the following line ranges from zero percent certainty to 100 percent certainty in the hierarchy of proof. Which of the following terms would Point C best describe?

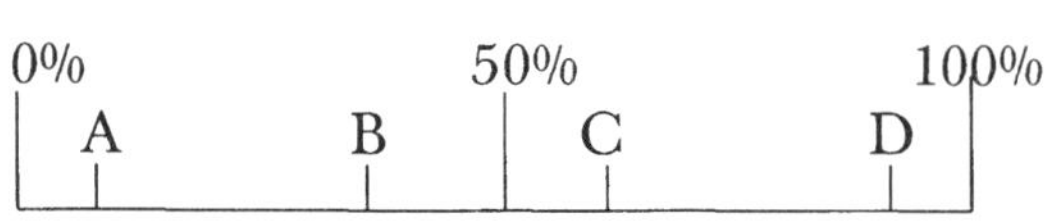

a. mere suspicion
b. probable cause
c. reasonable suspicion
d. proof beyond a reasonable doubt
e. none of the above

222. Continuing with the previous question, which of the following terms would Point D best describe?

a. proof beyond a reasonable doubt
b. probable cause
c. mere suspicion
d. reasonable suspicion
e. none of the above

223. Continuing with the previous question, which of the following terms would Point A best describe?

a. reasonable suspicion
b. mere suspicion
c. probable cause
d. proof beyond a reasonable doubt
e. none of the above

224. Continuing with the previous question, which of the following terms would Point B best describe?

a. mere suspicion
b. reasonable suspicion
c. probable cause
d. proof beyond a reasonable doubt
e. none of the above

225. Several inmates are eating supper in the dining hall when Jake enters the room. Jake walks up to one of the inmates and they exchange some harsh words. Suddenly, Jake reaches under his shirt, takes out a knife, and stabs the other person. One of the inmates, Morris, immediately interrupts his meal and tackles Jake, knocking the knife out of his hand. Morris then sits on Jake until corrections officers arrive. Which of the following best describes what Morris did in this situation?

a. citizen's arrest
b. false imprisonment
c. kidnapping
d. simple assault
e. simple battery

226. The elements of an arrest include:

a. the officer's intention to effect an arrest
b. the advising of "Miranda" rights immediately after the officer makes an arrest
c. an understanding by the person being arrested that it is the officer's intention to arrest him or her
d. only a & b above
e. only a & c above

227. Under what conditions may an officer make an bona fide arrest without an arrest warrant?

a. when someone has committed a felony or misdemeanor in the officer's jurisdiction

b. when someone has committed a misdemeanor within a reasonable period of time
c. when someone has committed a felony or misdemeanor in the officer's presence
d. when someone has committed an infraction outside the officer's presence
e. only when the officer is on duty and in uniform

228. Under which of the following conditions may an officer make a legitimate arrest for a misdemeanor that was NOT committed in the officer's presence?

a. when another officer holds an arrest warrant for the suspect
b. when the officer has a hunch that a warrant might possibly exist for the suspect's arrest
c. when the suspect is known to the officer
d. when the suspect is not known to the officer
e. when the suspect is known to the victim

229. Evaluate the following three statements:

1. One of the elements necessary for a criminal arrest is the actual or constructive seizure of the suspect.

2. An officer may make a bona fide warrantless arrest if a person commits a felony in the officer's presence and the officer has reasonable suspicion to believe this is the person who committed the crime.

3. The officer must have the arrest warrant in his or her hand at the actual time the officer seizes the suspect.

a. all three statements are false
b. only statements 1 & 2 are false
c. only statements 1 & 3 are false
d. only statements 2 & 3 are false
e. all three statements are true

230. Under which of the following conditions may an officer make a legitimate arrest without a warrant?

a. person committed a felony or misdemeanor in the presence of the officer
b. a felony has been committed and the officer has probable cause to believe that the person committed it
c. the officer has probable cause to believe that a felony has been or is being committed and reasonably believes that the person he or she is about to arrest has committed or is committing the crime
d. a warrant has been issued for the suspect
e. all of the above

231. Which of the following is the method of making an arrest with a warrant?

a. inform the person to be arrested of the cause of arrest
b. inform the person that a warrant has been issued
c. both of the above
d. neither of the above are needed

232. According to federal Supreme Court rulings, an officer must advise an arrested person of certain legal rights prior to engaging in any custodial interrogation or its equivalent. What are these rights called?

a. Miranda rights
b. Abelman rights
c. civil rights
d. criminal rights
e. inherent rights

233. What do the Miranda warnings generally address?

a. on-the-scene criminal investigation
b. bringing the accused before a magistrate without any unnecessary delay
c. advising a person of his or her rights any time an arrest is made
d. a custodial interrogation or its functional equivalent
e. advising a person of his or her rights any time the person is a suspect in a criminal case

234. Evaluate the following three statements:

1. A corrections officer may make a warrantless arrest for the violation of a county or municipal ordinance which is not committed in his or her presence.

2. A corrections officer must have probable cause to make an arrest.

3. "Miranda" rights must be administered whenever an officer has a suspect in custody, even though the officer has no intention of questioning the suspect.

a. all three statements are false
b. only statements 1 & 2 are false
c. only statements 1 & 3 are false
d. only statements 2 & 3 are false
e. all three statements are true

235. Evaluate the following three statements:

1. Although federal standards require that officers issue the "Miranda Rights Warning" prior to a custodial interrogation, Florida does not have such a requirement.

2. Arrest warrants shall be directed to all police chiefs, sheriffs, and wardens.

3. The "Miranda Warning" is only required during a felony investigation and not during a misdemeanor investigation.

a. all three statements are false
b. only statements 1 & 2 are false
c. only statements 1 & 3 are false
d. only statements 2 & 3 are false
e. all three statements are true

236. Under which of the following circumstances may a certified corrections officer make a bona fide arrest without a warrant?

a. a felony occurring in his or her presence
b. a misdemeanor occurring in his or her presence
c. a felony if probable cause has been established
d. a computer check reveals an outstanding warrant for the subject of the inquiry
e. all of the above

237. Which of the following terms best describes a written order issued by a law enforcement officer or a booking officer in lieu of a physical arrest that requires a person accused of violating the law to appear in a designated court or government office at a specified date and time?

a. trespass warning
b. notice to appear
c. habeas corpus
d. a writ
e. summary judgment

238. Which of the following must be present in order for a corrections officer to make a lawful search unless a recognized legal exception permits otherwise?

a. reasonable suspicion
b. probable cause
c. petit suspicion
d. grand suspicion
e. probable suspicion

239. Officer Terry arrests Brent for littering, handcuffs him, and transports him to jail. At the jail, Corrections Officer Johnson empties Brent's pockets, looks inside his backpack, and has Brent step out of his shoes. What doctrine allowed Officer Johnson to conduct this warrantless search?

a. Monroe
b. abandonment
c. incident to arrest
d. exigent circumstances
e. plain view

240. Continuing with the previous question, Officer Johnson looks inside Terry's hat and discovers a piece of paper that is crumpled up. When Officer Johnson opens the paper, he discovers four "crack rocks." What doctrine allowed Officer Johnson to conduct this warrantless search?

a. Monroe
b. abandonment
c. incident to arrest
d. exigent circumstances
e. plain view

241. Officer Schmidt is making the rounds and conducting a check on the inmates. As she rounds a corner, Officer Schmidt smells a pungent odor that, based upon her training and experience, she associates with marijuana. As she turns a corner, Officer Schmidt spots a woman standing with her back towards her. When Officer Schmidt says "Excuse me, ma'am," the woman turns around and Officer Schmidt observes what appears to be a rolled up cigarette in her hand. The woman immediately says, "Okay, you caught me smoking some dope!" Officer Schmidt immediately handcuffs the woman and puts out the burning cigarette-like object. What doctrine allowed Officer Schmidt to seize the burning cigarette-like object?

a. stop and frisk
b. abandonment
c. plain view

d. incident to arrest
e. exigent circumstances

242. Continuing with the previous question, the woman gets caught with a single joint of cannabis in her hand. Which of the following best describes this act?

a. trafficking in marijuana
b. possession of marijuana less than 20 grams
c. possession of marijuana more than 20 grams
d. possession of marijuana more than 99 grams
e. dealing in stolen property

243. How does Florida classify the crime possession of marijuana less than 20 grams?

a. a capital felony
b. a misdemeanor
c. a felony
d. an infraction
e. a civil breach

244. Which of the following terms best describes this statement: a voluntary agreement by a party in possession of, and exercising, sufficient authority and competency to permit a search?

a. stop and frisk
b. abandonment
c. incident to arrest
d. exigent circumstances
e. consent

245. Officer Mulvaney is walking down the corridor when he hears an inmate's voice coming from inside a room. The man is shouting "Don't kill me. Please don't kill me." Officer Mulvaney tries to open the door but it is locked. He then forces his way inside the closed door. What doctrine allowed Officer Mulvaney to enter the room uninvited?

a. exigent circumstances
a. stop and frisk
b. abandonment
c. incident to arrest
e. plain view

246. A corrections officer is conducting a search on an inmate who has returned from work-release. During the course of the search, the officer finds a three-inch long piece of copper tubing which is outfitted with a rubber grommet and some steel wool inside the tube. A visual inspection reveals some black residue and the suspect acknowledges that the object is a "crack pipe." Which of the following charges would be most appropriate?

a. possession of contraband
b. unlawful possession of a listed chemical
c. possession of cocaine
d. possession of drug paraphernalia
e. trafficking in cocaine

247. How does Florida classify the crime possession of drug paraphernalia?

a. a capital felony
b. a felony
c. an infraction
d. a misdemeanor
e. a civil breach

248. Officer Sims is patrolling along the fence line when he observes an inmate throwing rocks over the fence towards cars that are parked in the parking lot. At least one car has a broken windshield. What type of a crime is this?

a. criminal mischief
b. simple battery
c. aggravated battery
d. stalking
e. not a crime but a civil violation

249. Continuing with the previous question, Officer Sims yells "Hey! Stop!" to the inmate. The inmate sees Officer Sims approaching him. The inmate then turns away from Officer Sims and starts to run away from the officer. Officer Sims starts to chase the inmate and the inmate ducks into a building and looks for a place to hide. What type of a crime is this?

a. criminal mischief
b. simple battery
c. aggravated battery
d. stalking
e. obstruction of justice

250. As Officer Vasquez is walking through the recreation area, she observes an inmate using a can of spray paint to draw a gang symbol on the wall. What type of a violation is this?

a. criminal mischief
b. simple battery

c. aggravated battery
d. stalking
e. not a crime but an administrative violation

251. Which of the following terms best describes this situation?

a. misdemeanor
b. felony
c. civil infraction
d. administrative violation
e. regulatory violation

252. Inmate Suarez is using the pay telephone to talk to his wife. During the conversation, Mrs. Suarez tells her husband that she is divorcing him. The two argue briefly on the telephone before Mrs. Suarez hangs up on her husband. Inmate Suarez is so upset that he rips the receiver away from the telephone and then snatches the telephone off the wall and throws it on the floor. What type of a crime is this?

a. grand theft
b. aggravated battery
c. aggravated battery
d. criminal mischief
e. burglary

253. Continuing with the previous question, Officer Johnson observes Inmate Suarez throughout this entire incident. As Officer Johnson approaches Inmate Suarez, the inmate starts walking towards the officer. As Officer Johnson orders Inmate Suarez to stand still, but Inmate Suarez pushes the officer aside and says, "Get out of my way. I'm sick and tired of this place." What type of a crime is this?

a. simple assault
b. simple battery
c. aggravated assault
d. aggravated battery
e. criminal mischief

254. A person meets the criteria under F.S. 397 (Substance Abuse) for protective custody if he or she has lost the power of self-control with respect to substance use and what else?

a. has inflicted, has threatened to inflict, has attempted to inflict, or is likely to inflict physical harm on himself or herself unless admitted for care
b. needs substance abuse services but his or her judgment is so impaired by the substance abuse that he or she is incapable of appreciating the need for such services
c. both a & b are required to take into protective custody
d. either a or b alone is sufficient to take a person into protective custody
e. none of the above

255. Officer Schuler responds to a report of a possible suicide-in-progress. Upon arrival Officer Schuler finds Inmate Horton standing on the roof of a five-story building threatening to jump if anyone comes close. Eventually, the inmate surrenders to Officer Schuler and says that he is okay now and wants to go back to his cell. In addition to writing a report, what procedure should Officer Schuler follow?

a. arrest the inmate for filing a false police report
b. seek an involuntary commitment
c. send the inmate back to his cell and forget about the incident since no crime was committed
d. contact next-of-kin and have this person visit with the subject
e. contact the chaplain and have the chaplain counsel the inmate

256. How long can a person be detained at a receiving facility for an involuntary examination under the Florida Mental Health Act (Baker Act)?

a. 8 hours
b. 16 hours
c. 24 hours
d. 48 hours
e. 72 hours

257. Under what conditions may an officer take a person into protective custody?

a. has threatened to inflict bodily harm upon himself or herself
b. is incapable of taking care of himself or herself because of the underlying condition
c. has made threats to hurt another person
d. has injured himself or herself
e. all of the above

258. Which of the following acts is NOT included under obstruction of justice?

a. impersonating an officer
b. compounding felony
c. refusal to assist an officer
d. resisting an officer with violence
e. all are included

259. Florida Statutes define obstruction of justice as "actions, or lack of actions, which impair or prevent an officer from executing a legal process or duty." Which of the following actions would be considered obstruction of justice?

a. resisting an officer with or without violence while he or she is attempting to make an arrest
b. giving an officer a false identification card
c. running away from an officer to prevent being taken into custody
d. a visitor bringing a hacksaw blade inside the facility with the intent to pass the tool on to an inmate
e. all are considered obstruction of justice

260. "Obtaining money or any pecuniary advantage from someone or compelling that person to do any act or to refrain from doing any act against that person's will by threats of ill treatment, libelous accusations, or exposure of faults" describes which of the following crimes?

a. arson
b. assault
c. battery
d. forgery
e. extortion

261. What crime is it when a person tries to obtain money or other pecuniary benefit from someone else by threatening that person with ill treatment, libelous accusations, or exposure of some fault or dark secret?

a. 2nd degree theft
b. extortion
c. slander
d. libel
e. assault

262. A person who willfully and unlawfully, or while in the commission of any felony, by fire or explosion, damages or causes to be damaged any dwelling or its contents has committed which of the following crimes?

a. criminal mischief
b. assault
c. arson
d. obstruction of justice
e. vandalism

263. How does Florida classify arson?

a. a capital felony
b. an infraction
c. a felony
d. a misdemeanor
e. a civil breach

264. Pulling a fire alarm when, in fact, there is no fire to report is classified as what?

a. an infraction
b. a misdemeanor
c. a capital felony
d. a felony
e. a civil breach

265. Which of the following items is NOT included in the term "structure" when dealing with arson?

a. a carport
b. a tent
c. any building
d. a vehicle
e. all are included in the term "structure"

266. Any person who willfully or unreasonably interferes with, hinders, assaults, or attempts to interfere with or hinder, any firefighter in the performance of his duty commits what type of a crime?

a. an infraction
b. a misdemeanor
c. a civil breach
d. a capital felony
e. a felony

267. If a person deliberately sets fire to a building in the hopes of killing someone who is inside, that crime is classified as what?

a. a felony
b. an infraction
c. a misdemeanor

d. a capital felony
e. a civil breach

268. What is the definition of the legal term "assault?"

a. a threat by word or act to do violence to the person of another, coupled with the apparent ability to carry out the threat, and intended to create a well-founded fear that violence is imminent
b. accidentally touching, striking, or causing bodily harm to another person against that person's will
c. a trespassing combined with a battery
d. intentionally touching, striking, or causing bodily harm to another person against that person's will
e. none of the above

269. What is the definition of the legal term "battery?"

a. a threat by word or act to do violence to the person of another, coupled with the apparent ability to carry out the threat
b. accidentally touching, striking, or causing bodily harm to another person against that person's will
c. verbal threats or acts intended to create a well-founded fear that violence is imminent
d. intentionally touching, striking, or causing bodily harm to another person against that person's will
e. none of the above

270. Which of the following conditions must be present to justify an arrest for battery on a corrections officer?

a. the officer must have been in uniform
b. the violator must have known that the battery was on an officer and the officer was acting in the "line of duty"
c. the officer must have warned the violator that a battery on an officer is a felony
d. the violator must have been resisting arrest when the battery occurred
e. all of the above

271. Normally, a battery is classified as a misdemeanor. However, if a battery is committed on certain people, then the incident is automatically elevated to a felony. Battery against which of the following categories of victims automatically produces a felony charge?

a. a child
b. a firefighter
c. an infant
d. a priest
e. spouse

272. As you walk into a laundry area, you observe one inmate use her fist to strike another inmate in the stomach. What is the most appropriate charge in this instance?

a. aggravated assault
b. aggravated battery
c. simple assault
d. simple battery
e. vandalism

273. What criminal violation is described by the following elements?

- One person threatens to harm another person
- There is an apparent ability to carry the threat out
- The violence is imminent
- The victim is afraid that violence will occur

a. petty theft
b. grand theft
c. simple assault
d. simple battery
e. robbery

274. What constitutes any intentional touching, no matter how slight, if the person is touched against his or her will?

a. assault
b. attempted assault
c. attempted battery
d. battery
e. malfeasance

275. Which of the following offenses is classified as a felony?

a. assault on a corrections officer
b. battery
c. battery on a spouse
d. disorderly intoxication
e. aggravated assault

276. What term is defined as "committing battery and intentionally or knowingly causing great bodily harm, permanent disability, or permanent disfigurement or using a deadly weapon?"

a. aggravated battery
b. aggravated assault
c. simple assault
d. simple battery
e. battery on a corrections officer

277. How does Florida generally classify a simple assault or a simple battery?

a. an infraction
b. a misdemeanor
c. a capital felony
d. a felony
e. a civil breach

278. Which of the following conditions is required under the aggravated assault statute?

a. great bodily harm
b. a deadly weapon
c. at least one witness to the event for verification
d. serious injury
e. a & c above

279. Inmate Connors and Inmate Nims both work in the kitchen area as cooks. Connors is mad at Nims for some unknown reason. While Nims is snoozing in a chair in a corner of the kitchen area, Connors pours a pot of boiling water on Nims causing severe burns to the arms and chest area. What is the appropriate charge against Connors?

a. aggravated assault
b. aggravated battery
c. battery
d. battery on a spouse
e. none of the above

280. Officer Douglas is working the outer gate to a corrections facility on visitation day. Sally drives up to the gate intending to visit her boyfriend Ralph. However, Officer Douglas advises Sally that Ralph is on restriction and is not allowed to have any visitors that day. Sally becomes quite upset with this news. Sally becomes verbally abusive towards Officer Douglas, swings her purse at Officer Douglas, but misses and fails to make contact. Officer Douglas takes Sally into custody without further incident and charges Sally with simple assault on a corrections officer. What type of an offense is this charge?

a. infraction
b. misdemeanor
c. felony
d. big mistake (F.S. 999.99)
e. civil breach

281. Aggravated battery results:

a. when a deadly weapon is used
b. only if the victim is under 18 years old
c. when the victim suffers great bodily harm or permanent disfigurement
d. all of the above
e. a or c above only

282. Inmate Peters threatens to hit Inmate Knight with the iron pipe that Peters is holding in his hand unless Knight moves out of his way. What type of a crime is this?

a. simple assault
b. simple battery
c. aggravated battery
d. aggravated assault
e. attempted murder

283. Evaluate the following statements:

1. Assault is the actual, completed act when the threat has been carried out.

2. A battery is excusable for officers when preventing offenses or serious injury.

3. An officer may not use any force to take a person deemed to be in need of substance abuse services to a hospital or a licensed detoxification or addictions receiving facility.

a. all three statements are false
b. only statements 1 & 2 are false
c. only statements 1 & 3 are false
d. only statements 2 & 3 are false
e. all three statements are true

284. Punching another person in the arm would be an example of what type of crime?

a. simple assault
b. aggravated assault
c. simple battery
d. aggravated battery

e. resisting with violence

285. Threatening to hit another person with the baseball bat that one is holding would be an example of what type of a crime?

a. simple assault
b. aggravated assault
c. simple battery
d. aggravated battery
e. resisting with violence

286. Under Florida law, prostitution is what?

a. illegal, but should not be enforced
b. the giving or receiving of the body for sexual activity for hire
c. a felony
d. all of the above
e. b & c above

287. Florida Statutes defines sexual battery as what type of penetration by, or union with, the sexual organ of another or the anal or vaginal penetration of another by any other object?

a. oral
b. anal
c. vaginal
d. all of the above
e. b & c above only

288. Which of the following refers to making indecent advances towards children in order to obtain sexual gratification?

a. exhibitionism
b. prostitution
c. child molestation
d. pornography
e. obstruction

289. Inmate Paul has a habit of dropping his pants and underwear down to his ankles whenever a visitor walks by him. What type of a crime is this activity?

a. prostitution
b. molestation
c. pornography
d. obstruction
e. indecent exposure

290. How does Florida classify a sexual battery incident if the victim is under the age of 12 and the offender is 18 years old or over?

a. an infraction
b. a misdemeanor
c. a civil breach
d. a capital felony
e. a life felony

291. How does Florida classify a sexual battery incident if the victim is under the age of 12 and the offender under the age of 18?

a. a capital felony
b. an infraction
c. a misdemeanor
d. a life felony
e. a civil breach

292. Which of the following are the elements that constitute sexual battery?

a. lack of consent from the victim
b. union with the sex organ of another
c. forces the victim to submit
d. all of the above
e. a & b only

293. Usually sexual battery is a second-degree felony. However, if certain circumstances are present, then the offense is elevated automatically to a first-degree felony. Which of the following is one of those aggravating conditions?

a. the victim is elderly
b. the victim and the offender are of the same race
c. the victim and the offender are of different races
d. the offender administered a narcotic or intoxicant without the knowledge or consent of the victim
e. the offender is mentally defective

294. Under what circumstances does Florida permit mandatory AIDS testing to be performed in sexual battery cases?

a. on persons who witnessed a sexual battery
b. on persons who were sexually battered
c. on persons charged with sexual battery
d. on persons who investigate sexual battery
e. on persons convicted of sexual battery

295. The taking of money or property from the custody of another person, with the intent to deprive the person or owner of the money or property either permanently or temporarily, through the use of force, violence, assault, or putting in fear refers to which of the following offenses?

a. theft
b. arson
c. robbery
d. carjacking
e. criminal mischief

296. How does Florida generally classify a robbery?

a. a capital felony
b. a felony
c. an infraction
d. a misdemeanor
e. a civil breach

297. What is the incident called if a person commits a robbery with some type of a weapon?

a. strong-armed robbery
b. larceny from a person
c. grand larceny
d. armed robbery
e. none of the above

298. What is the incident called if a person commits a robbery without using a weapon?

a. strong-armed robbery
b. armed robbery
c. larceny from a person
d. grand larceny
e. petty larceny

299. Ms. Abernathy is walking down the street carrying her purse in her hand. Her purse contains $545 in cash. When Ms. Abernathy reaches the corner, the suspect runs past her and yanks on Ms. Abernathy's purse. The jolt causes Ms. Abernathy to fall to the ground and she releases her grip on the purse. What type of a crime has taken place?

a. armed robbery
b. larceny from a person
c. grand larceny
d. petty larceny
e. strong-armed robbery

300. Ms. Whitney is out shopping for clothes. Her purse contains $545 in cash. Ms. Whitney sets her purse down on the counter while she looks at some clothes. When she turns around, Ms. Whitney discovers her purse is missing. What type of a crime has taken place?

a. strong-armed robbery
b. grand larceny
c. petty larceny
d. armed robbery
e. larceny from a person

301. Ms. Kelly is out shopping for clothes. Her purse contains $545 in cash. Ms. Kelly sets her purse down on the counter while she looks at some clothes. As Ms. Kelly turns around, both she and the suspect pick up her purse at the same time. The suspect yanks on the purse and Ms. Kelly falls to the floor, but Ms. Kelly manages to hang on to the purse and starts to scream for help. The suspect pulls on the purse again, but Ms. Kelly does not let go of it. The suspect, fearing apprehension, lets go of the purse and runs away. What type of a crime has taken place?

a. attempted armed robbery
b. attempted strong-armed robbery
c. attempted larceny from a person
d. attempted grand larceny
e. attempted petty larceny

302. Mr. Jackson, the driver of a vehicle, is stopped at a traffic light. A suspect walks up to the car, points a gun at Mr. Jackson's head, and orders him to exit the car. Mr. Jackson complies and the suspect gets into the car and drives away. What type of a crime has taken place?

a. grand larceny
b. strong-armed robbery
c. armed robbery
d. larceny from a person
e. carjacking

303. What does Florida call a robbery that takes place when a suspect enters a dwelling and then robs the inhabitants?

a. strong-armed robbery
b. armed robbery
c. home-invasion robbery
d. larceny from a person
e. homejacking

304. A police officer is walking down the street when suddenly a man runs out of a house and starts to shoot a gun at the officer. The officer returns fire and one bullet strikes the assailant killing him instantly. What type of a homicide has taken place?

a. justifiable homicide
b. manslaughter
c. first-degree murder
d. excusable homicide
e. third-degree murder

305. A homicide committed by accident and misfortune when doing any lawful act by lawful means with usual ordinary caution, and without any unlawful intent is classified as what in Florida?

a. first-degree murder
b. justifiable homicide
c. manslaughter
d. third-degree murder
e. excusable homicide

306. A homicide that takes place when a person is resisting any attempt to murder him or her would be classified as what in Florida?

a. first-degree murder
b. excusable homicide
c. manslaughter
d. justifiable homicide
e. third-degree murder

307. A man walks into a convenience store, points a gun at the clerk, and demands all the money from the till. The clerk can see that the robber is extremely nervous and sweating profusely. The gun goes off unexpectedly and the suspect yells, "I'm sorry. I didn't mean to shoot you. It went off by itself." The clerk dies at the scene. What type of a homicide has taken place?

a. excusable homicide
b. justifiable homicide
c. manslaughter
d. third-degree murder
e. first-degree murder

308. List six different types of homicide contained in Florida law?

1.

2.

3.

4.

5.

6.

309. List six offenses that pertain to the felony-murder rule?

1.

2.

3.

4.

5.

6.

310. Evaluate the following three statements:

1. Florida still recognizes the common law rule of evidence known as the "year-and-a-day" rule.

2. Premeditation refers to the religious act of praying to God.

3. A females cannot be the victim of manslaughter.

a. all three statements are false
b. only statements 1 & 2 are false
c. only statements 1 & 3 are false
d. only statements 2 & 3 are false
e. all three statements are true

311. Evaluate the following three statements:

1. Helping somebody commit suicide is a felony in Florida.

2. A person who is driving under the influence of alcoholic beverages and who strikes and kills a pedestrian can be charged with first-degree murder.

3. The Florida homicide statutes contains a separate charged known as "vessel homicide."

a. all three statements are true
b. only statements 1 & 2 are true
c. only statements 1 & 3 are true
d. only statements 2 & 3 are true
e. all three statements are false

312. What type of an offense is vehicular homicide?

a. misdemeanor
b. felony
c. an infraction
d. civil breach
e. none of the above

313. What crime does a person commit if he or she knowingly obtains or uses, or endeavors to obtain or to use, the property of another with intent to, either temporarily or permanently, deprive the other person of a right to the property or a benefit therefrom?

a. burglary
b. robbery
c. larceny
d. trespass
e. criminal mischief

314. What amount of money is the dividing line between a petty theft and a grand theft in Florida?

a. $100
b. $200
c. $250
d. $300
e. $500

315. Stealing certain objects in Florida, no matter what the object is really worth, is automatically a felony. Which of the following does NOT belong on that list?

a. 1,000 pieces of citrus
b. a cow
c. a firearm
d. a fire extinguisher
e. a will

316. Which of the following does NOT constitute "retail theft?"

a. altering or removing a price tag
b. stealing a book from the library
c. taking a shopping cart from the premises to use at home
d. transferring merchandise from one container to another
e. taking merchandise without paying for same

317. Evaluate the following three statements:

1. If a person buys a twenty-inch color television still in the box for $99 in cash only off the back dock of a department store, it would be reasonable to assume that he or she should have known the merchandise was stolen.

2. Stealing $50 worth of lumber from a properly marked construction site is a felony.

3. Using false identification to rent a car gives rise to an inference that the vehicle was obtained with intent to commit theft.

a. all three statements are true
b. only statements 1 & 2 are true
c. only statements 1 & 3 are true
d. only statements 2 & 3 are true
e. all three statements are false

318. How does Florida generally classify dealing in stolen property?

a. an infraction
b. a misdemeanor
c. a capital felony
d. a felony
e. a civil breach

319. Evaluate the following statements:

1. Stealing an item which is worth $734.57 would be an example of grand theft.

2. Theft or larceny is generally defined as taking by force or the threat of force of property belonging to another person with the intent to permanently deprive.

3. Stealing a "midnight special" gun worth $69.95 is a misdemeanor.

a. all three statements are false
b. only statements 1 & 2 are false
c. only statements 1 & 3 are false
d. only statements 2 & 3 are false
e. all three statements are true

320. Homer is an inmate assigned to working in the garage area. At the end of the shift, Homer slips a screwdriver into his back pocket and then leaves the work area to return to his cell. Officer Horne saw Homer steal the screwdriver. Officer Horne follows Homer outside the garage and places Homer under arrest. While Officer Horne is handcuffing Homer, Homer begins to cry and sobs, "I didn't really mean to steal the screwdriver." Later at trial, Homer's attorney asks the judge to rule that the arrest is invalid because Officer Horne did not Mirandize Homer before taking him into custody. If you were the presiding judge, how would you rule?

a. unlawful arrest – not the functional equivalent of custodial interrogation
b. unlawful arrest – the functional equivalent of a custodial interrogation
c. lawful arrest – not the functional equivalent of a custodial interrogation
d. lawful arrest – the functional equivalent of a custodial interrogation

321. Continuing with the previous question, Homer's attorney asks the court to suppress Homer's statement "I didn't really mean to steal the screwdriver" since Officer Horne had not issued any Miranda warnings. If you were the presiding judge, how would you rule?

a. statement admissible – not the functional equivalent of a custodial interrogation
b. statement admissible – the functional equivalent of a custodial interrogation
c. statement not admissible – not the functional equivalent of a custodial interrogation
d. statement not admissible – the functional equivalent of a custodial interrogation

322. Continuing further with the previous question, Homer's attorney asks the court to suppress Homer's arrest because Officer Horne was not readily visible to inmates in the garage area. In fact, Homer testifies that he was entrapped. Had he known Officer Horne was watching him, Homer stated that he never would have stolen the screwdriver. If you were the presiding judge, how would you rule?

a. unlawful arrest – entrapment
b. unlawful arrest – officer not on duty at the time
c. unlawful arrest – officer not readily identifiable as a police officer
d. lawful arrest

Chapter 2 Answer Key

1. D
2. C
3. C
4. E
5. B
6. E
7. A
8. A
9. A
10.C

11. E
12. C
13. B
14. B
15. A
16. C
17. E
18. A
19. A
20. B

21. E
22. E
23. E
24. A
25. C
26. D
27. D
28. C
29. B
30. C

31. D
32. D
33. B
34. B
35. A
36. C
37. D
38. A
39. B
40. C

41. D
42. B
43. D
44. B
45. B
46. A
47. C
48. E
49. E
50. D

51. C
52. B
53. E
54. A
55. C
56. E
57. C
58. A
59. C
60. A

61. B
62. E
63. D
64. D
65. C
66. C
67. C
68. C
69. D
70. D

71. A
72. D
73. B
74. D
75. A
76. E
77. D
78. B
79. D
80. C

81. D
82. B
83. C
84. A
85. A
86. B
87. C
88. A
89. D
90. A

91. D
92. B
93. C
94. D
95. E
96. D
97. E
98. D
99. B
100. A

101. E
102. B
103. C
104. C
105. B
106. C
107. A
108. C
109. C
110. C

111. C
112. D
113. D
114. E
115. B
116. B
117. D
118. A
119. D
120. E

121. E
122. B
123. A
124. B
125. E
126. A
127. D
128. D
129. E
130. E

131. C
132. C
133. B
134. B
135. E
136. D
137. B
138. C
139. D
140. A

141. B
142. A
143. B
144. D
145. D
146. D
147. C
148. C
149. A
150. C

151. D
152. E
153. A
154. B
155. E
156. D
157. B
158. E
159. A
160. E

161. B
162. D
163. B
164. D
165. E
166. D
167. D
168. B
169. B
170. A

171. C
172. B
173. D
174. A
175. E
176. E
177. B
178. C
179. B
180. D

181. A
182. D
183. E
184. A
185. C
186. D
187. D
188. B
189. B
190. A

191. C
192. D
193. E
194. D
195. D
196. E
197. B
198. B
199. D
200. A

201. B
202. A
203. C
204. E
205. D
206. E
207. E
208. A
209. A
210. A

211. C
212. D
213. C
214. C
215. D
216. C
217. B
218. B
219. E
220. B

221. B
222. A
223. B
224. B
225. A
226. E
227. C
228. A
229. D
230. E

231. C
232. A
233. D
234. C
235. A
236. E
237. B
238. B
239. C
240. C

241. C
242. B
243. B
244. E
245. A
246. D
247. D
248. A
249. E
250. A

251. A
252. D
253. B
254. D
255. B
256. E
257. E
258. E
259. E
260. E

261. B
262. C
263. C
264. D
265. E
266. E
267. A
268. A
269. D
270. B

271. B
272. D
273. C
274. D
275. E
276. A
277. B
278. B
279. B
280. B

281. E
282. D
283. C
284. C
285. B
286. B
287. D
288. C
289. E
290. D

291. D
292. D
293. D
294. C
295. C
296. B
297. D
298. A
299. E
300. B

301. B
302. E
303. C
304. A
305. E
306. D
307. E
308. *
309. *
310. A

311. C
312. B
313. C
314. D
315. A
316. B
317. A
318. D
319. D
320. C

321. A
322. D

Answers to "List Questions"

308. (1) 1st-degree murder
(2) 2nd-degree murder
(3) 3rd-degree murder
(4) manslaughter
(5) vehicular homicide
(6) assisting self-murder
(7) killing of unborn child by injury to mother
(8) unnecessary killing to prevent unlawful act
(9) justifiable homicide
(10) excusable homicide
(11) vessel homicide

309. (1) trafficking in drugs and controlled substances
(2) arson
(3) sexual battery
(4) robbery
(5) burglary
(6) kidnapping
(7) escape
(8) aggravated cild abuse
(9) aircraft piracy
(10) unlawful throwing, placing, or discharging of a destructive device or bomb
(11) carjacking
(12) home-invasion robbery
(13) aggravated abuse of an elderly person or disabled adult
(14) aggravated stalking
(15) murder of another human being
(16) resisting an officer with violence
(17) felony terrorism

CHAPTER 3

INTERPERSONAL SKILLS I

Chapter Overview

This part of your test preparation focuses upon basic interpersonal skills. As the following topical listing indicates, corrections officers have become increasingly aware that the constituency with whom they interact consists of a very broad and diverse spectrum. A number of studies show that corrections officers spend a considerable amount of their energies addressing noncriminal matters. Thus, it is very important for corrections officers to become skilled in dealing with inmates.

A look at the goals and learning objectives that the basic recruit curriculum devotes to this area reveals the following concerns that are reflected in the test preparation questions:

- Courtesy
- Human Behavior/Human Needs
- Juvenile and Youthful Offenders
- Human Diversity
- Persons with Mental Disorders
- Mentally Retarded Persons
- Physically Handicapped Persons
- Recognizing and Responding to Substance Abusers
- Crisis Intervention Techniques
- Stress Recognition and Reduction
- Suicide Prevention and Intervention

Questions

1. Which of the following offers the best definition of courtesy?

   a. an attitude that values consideration, but not necessarily cooperation
   b. the demonstration of consideration, cooperation, and respect when interacting with others
   c. a demeanor appropriate to the situation
   d. friendliness
   d. consideration, positioning, cooperation when appropriate

2. Which of the following are methods that an officer can use to demonstrate courtesy?

   a. tone of voice
   b. mannerisms
   c. close attention to his or her personal budget
   d. body language
   e. only a, b & d above

3. Why is courtesy an important element of criminal justice work?

   a. image reflects on your agency
   b. it creates support for other officers and you
   c. it reflects self-respect
   d. public relations
   e. all of the above

4. Officers who use an officious and oppressive manner, an overbearing tone of voice, or negative body language will probably generate what type of a result?

   a. an indifferent response from people they encounter
   b. added support for officers from people they encounter
   c. a positive response from people they encounter
   d. a negative response from people they encounter
   e. b & c above only

5. Which of the following is NOT a basic principle when taking telephone calls?

   a. proper use of the alpha-numeric code
   b. prompt answering
   c. courteous termination of call
   d. appropriate interest and sincerity
   e. quick and accurate routing of calls

6. Evaluate the following statements:

   1. In order to calm a hysterical phone caller, it is important to talk much louder than the caller, so that he or she can hear you.
   2. If a caller is put in a good psychological mood, it will be easier for you to obtain information.
   3. Since radio communications are considered "secure" communications, it is allowable to transmit classified information by this medium.

   a. all three statements are false
   b. only statements 1 & 2 are false
   c. only statements 1 & 3 are false
   d. only statements 2 & 3 are false
   e. all three statements are true

7. Which of the following terms refers to a caller who is overly humorous?

   a. angry caller
   b. hysterical caller
   c. gossipy caller
   d. facetious caller
   e. tempting caller

8. Which of the following is NOT a basic quality of voice control that should be used in telephone conversation?

   a. alertness
   b. expressiveness
   c. pleasantness
   d. distinctness
   e. sarcasm

9. Being firm, pleasant, calm, and maintaining a polite tone of voice would best be used when trying to control which type of caller?

   a. angry caller
   b. hysterical caller
   c. gossipy caller
   d. foreign language caller
   e. facetious caller

10. The first needs to be satisfied are referred to as what?

    a. safety needs
    b. basic needs
    c. selfish desires
    d. animal instincts
    e. relationship needs

11. Evaluate the following statements:

    1. Individuals normally set priorities in their needs. Higher order needs (i.e., self-actualization needs) are met first. Lower order needs (i.e., basic safety) are not usually met until higher order needs are met.

    2. Individual motivation can be positive or negative depending on the need to be met.

    3. Persons suffering from mental disorders often display self-destructive or violent behavior and sudden unprovoked attacks on others.

    a. all three statements are false
    b. only statements 1 & 2 are false
    c. only statements 1 & 3 are false
    d. only statements 2 & 3 are false
    e. only statement 1 is false

12. In terms of inmate behavior, the need to assert individuality may manifest itself in aggressive or criminal behavior. Under which category in the hierarchy of needs would this type of behavior fall?

    a. basic needs
    b. belongingness
    c. ego-status
    d. self-actualization
    e. safety

13. In terms of officer behavior, the need to strive to improve one's self through education and training would fall under which category in the hierarchy of needs?

    a. basic needs
    b. belongingness
    c. ego-status
    d. self-actualization
    e. safety

14. Evaluate the following statements:

    1. Individual motivation can be positive or negative depending on the need to be met.

    2. According to the hierarchy of needs theory, the need to belong is not a basic need.

    3. Correctional officers, by virtue of the positions they hold in the institution, do not have any needs that can be fulfilled in that environment.

    a. all three statements are true
    b. only statements 1 & 2 are true
    c. only statements 1 & 3 are true
    d. only statements 2 & 3 are true
    e. all three statements are false

15. Characteristics of juvenile offenders often include which of the following?

    a. high degree of responsibility
    b. unpredictable behavior patterns
    c. usually come from upper income families
    d. seldom question authority
    e. very submissive

16. Evaluate the following statements:

    1. When dealing with juvenile offenders, a law enforcement officer must arrest and transport to juvenile detention any offender charged with an offense that would be criminal if the juvenile were an adult.

    2. Most juvenile delinquents go on to become adult offenders.

    3. The public records requirement that appears in Florida Statutes 119.07 F.S. (inspection and examination of records; exemptions) applies to the press as well as to private citizens.

    a. all three statements are false
    b. only statements 1 & 2 are false
    c. only statements 1 & 3 are false
    d. only statements 2 & 3 are false
    e. all three statements are true

17. Which of the following characteristics does NOT characterize youthful offenders?

    a. may come from a broken home
    b. high degree of irresponsibility
    c. unpredictable behavior patterns
    d. defiant, no realization of seriousness of actions or consequences
    e. all of the above

18. Evaluate the following statements:

    1. Juvenile inmates are more motive-oriented while adult inmates are more impulsive.

    2. One purpose behind juvenile corrections is to plan, develop, and implement correctional programs and services for the individual.

    3. One reason why juveniles are treated differently from adults in correctional facilities is to give juveniles access to opportunities for normal growth and development.

a. all three statements are true
b. only statements 1 & 2 are true
c. only statements 1 & 3 are true
d. only statements 2 & 3 are true
e. all three statements are false

19. A model corrections officer who works with juvenile inmates should possess which of the following characteristics?

a. patience
b. good humor
c. understanding
d. self-control
e. all of the above

20. Which of the following is NOT a formal disciplinary action when working with juvenile inmates?

a. individual one-on-one counseling
b. probation
c. extra duty
d. loss of gain time
e. confinement

21. Evaluate the following statements:

1. Suicide is one of the leading causes of death for juveniles.

2. Quite often, juvenile inmates are more "playful" than adult inmates.

3. A key aspect of a corrections officer's job is to serve as a role model for juvenile inmates.

a. all three statements are true
b. only statements 1 & 2 are true
c. only statements 1 & 3 are true
d. only statements 2 & 3 are true
e. all three statements are false

22. Which of the considerations listed below would NOT apply when dealing with members of different ethnic groups?

a. religion
b. personal space
c. appearance
d. dietary difference
e. language difference

23. Persons defined as a "cultural group" will share all of the following characteristics EXCEPT which one?

a. social class
b. material traits
c. customary beliefs
d. social forms
e. gestures and manners

24. "A set of learned behaviors, values, beliefs, and patterns of interaction shared by a group of people who tend to share historical and/or geographical proximity" defines which of the following terms?

a. ethnicity
b. culture
c. race
d. minority ethnocentric
e. prejudice

25. Which of the following terms refers to people who share common traits of history, national origin, and cultural patterns?

a. ethnicity
b. culture
c. race
d. minority ethnocentric
e. prejudice

26. Which of the following words refers to the situation where a persons believes that his or her own group is superior to other social groups?

a. ethnicity
b. culture
c. race
d. ethnocentric
e. prejudice

27. ________ is the broadest classification of people. It includes geographical, national, or ethnic groups who share common physical characteristics.

a. ethnicity
b. culture
c. race
d. ethnocentric
e. prejudice

28. Cultural attributes could be identified as which of the following?

a. cultural values, spiritual beliefs, thinking patterns

b. family behavior/roles, communication style
c. race characteristics
d. all of the above
e. a & b above only

29. Evaluate the following statements with regard to the attributes of culture:

1. differences facilitate communication
2. differences are barriers to communication
3. similarities facilitate communication
4. similarities are barriers to communication

a. all above statements are true
b. statements 1 & 4 are true
c. statements 1 & 3 are true
d. statements 2 & 3 are true
e. statements 2 & 4 are true

30. List seven techniques that are helpful in building rapport and trust in a diverse cultural setting.

1.

2.

3.

4.

5.

6.

7.

31. Which of the following refers to the negative stress humans experience when they are removed from their native culture and placed in a culturally different environment without the skills to cope with the change?

a. discrimination
b. culture shock
c. prejudice
d. cultural effectiveness
e. ethnicity

32. Which of the following refers to the capacity to recognize cultural attributes and use information gathered to function effectively within any given culture?

a. discrimination
b. culture shock
c. dominant culture
d. cultural effectiveness
e. ethnicity

33. Which of the following refers to those values, beliefs, and patterns of learned behavior that are intrinsic to the society in which people from various cultures must function?

a. discrimination
b. culture shock
c. dominant culture
d. cultural effectiveness
e. ethnicity

34. A set of expected beliefs, values, learned behaviors that are promoted and perpetuated by a majority of the members and institutions of a given society refers to which of the following?

a. discrimination
b. culture shock
c. dominant culture
d. cultural effectiveness
e. ethnicity

35. Two people of the same race can be born into different groups. For example, one black person may be a Jamaican-American while another may be an African-American. Which of the following terms refers to this distinction?

a. ethnocentric
b. ethnicity
c. prejudice
d. stereotype
e. minority

36. Which of the following terms is the opposite of the word "majority?"

a. ethnocentric
b. ethnicity
c. prejudice
d. stereotype
e. minority

37. Prejudgment of a person, situation, or group is known as what?

a. ethnocentrizing
b. ethnicity
c. prejudice

d. stereotyping
e. culture judgment

38. Which of the following behaviors stems from prejudice?

a. discrimination
b. ethnicity
c. ethnocentrizing
d. stereotyping
e. culture

39. Which of the following terms refers to an exaggerated belief associated with a particular group, the function of which is to justify or rationalize one's attitude and conduct towards members of that group?

a. ethnocentrizing
b. ethnicity
c. prejudice
d. stereotype
e. culture judgment

40. Effective communication:

a. is the state in which one has developed the capacity to appreciate other cultures
b. is the process of sending and receiving a message with the least possible loss of meaning
c. is based on the overgeneralization and value judgment of one culture over another and is useless in understanding diverse cultures
d. essentially is the same thing as ethnocentrizing
e. all of the above

41. Stereotyping refers to which of the following?

a. is the state in which one has developed the capacity to appreciate other cultures
b. occurs with gender as well as ethnicity or race
c. is based on the over-generalization and value judgment of one culture over another and is useless in understanding diverse cultures
d. essentially is ethnocentrizing
e. b & c above

42. To become culturally effective, one must be aware of cultural attributes. Cultural attributes fall into five categories. What are these categories?

a. values and assumptions, spiritual beliefs, family behavior patterns or roles, criminal records, and thinking patterns
b. values and assumptions, spiritual beliefs, family behavior patterns or roles, communication style, and thinking patterns
c. values and assumptions, spiritual beliefs, family behavior patterns or roles, communication style, and economic status
d. educational level, spiritual beliefs, family behavior patterns or roles, communication style, and thinking patterns
e. values and assumptions, spiritual beliefs, family behavior patterns or roles, educational level, and thinking patterns

43. Evaluate the following statements:

1. The culturally effective person must focus on and recognize differences in communication methods to be able to prevent them from becoming communication barriers.

2. Bridging cultural barriers is an acquired skill requiring both self-awareness and respect and understanding for others and their cultural values and assumptions.

3. When encountering other cultures, one must be aware of cultural differences in behavioral styles, as well as verbal and nonverbal communication styles.

a. all three statements are true
b. only statements 1 & 2 are true
c. only statements 2 & 3 are true
d. only statements 1 & 3 are true
e. all three statements are false

44. Evaluate the following statements:

1. Culture resource persons can help us learn culture more quickly.

2. Culture shock may occur when one's ability to communicate cross-culturally is so severely limited that his or her own cultural identity is threatened.

3. Becoming culturally effective seldom helps us prevent our own culture shock.

a. all three statements are true
b. only statements 1 & 2 are true
c. only statements 2 & 3 are true
d. only statements 1 & 3 are true
e. all three statements are false

45. Stereotypes do not define cultures because they are derived from:

a. value judgment
b. cultural ignorance
c. failure to take individual variation into account
d. all of the above
e. b & c above only

46. Which of the following refers to that which the people of a culture hold to be sacred and important, and from which all other cultural attributes are derived?

a. cultural values
b. spiritual or religious beliefs
c. family roles or behavior patterns
d. stereotypes
e. ethnocentrism

47. The belief in the existence or nonexistence of a Supreme Being and whether or not there is an afterlife are example of which of the following?

a. cultural values
b. spiritual or religious beliefs
c. family roles or behavior patterns
d. stereotypes
e. cultural remnants

48. Evaluate the following statements:

1. Traditional cultural roles are shaped by cultural values and spiritual beliefs.

2. Roles strongly impact the dynamics of interactions within the family.

3. Roles can be displayed and emphasized in the ways that the people of a given culture dress.

a. all three statements are true
b. only statements 1 & 2 are true
c. only statements 2 & 3 are true
d. only statements 1 & 3 are true
e. all three statements are false

49. Evaluate the following statements:

1. Thinking patterns are strongly influenced by values, spiritual beliefs and behavior patterns.

2. Emotions may play a larger role in the thinking processes of some groups than in others.

3. All cultural groups will be deductive thinkers.

a. all three statements are true
b. only statements 1 & 2 are true
c. only statements 2 & 3 are true
d. only statements 1 & 3 are true
e. all three statements are false

50. Evaluate the following statements:

1. Communication patterns consist of the culture's recurring communication techniques of both a verbal and nonverbal nature.

2. Dialect, slang, body language, and gestures are not considered subsets of communication within a given culture.

3. Important subsets of communication patterns are the culture's art, music, dance, and dress. Art, music, and dance are all creative ways that the people of a culture express their thoughts, ideas, feelings, and perceptions.

a. all three statements are true
b. only statements 1 & 2 are true
c. only statements 2 & 3 are true
d. only statements 1 & 3 are true
e. all three statements are false

51. Listening skills must be developed because there are so many impeding factors such as:

a. being more concerned with what we want to say than what is being said to us
b. hearing only what we want to hear
c. preconceived notions about what the speaker is saying or is going to say
d. assumptions and values that alter the meaning of the words between the speaker and the listener
e. all of the above

52. The six guidelines for bridging barriers are:

1. Listening effectively.
2. Interject bias wherever possible.
3. Monitoring perception.
4. No risk-taking.
5. Cultivating self-awareness.
6. Taking risks.
7. Be judgmental.
8. Seeking feedback.
9. Resisting judgmental reactions.

a. 1, 2, 4, 5, 6, & 7 are correct
b. 1, 3, 5, 6, 8, & 9 are correct
c. 2, 3, 5, 6, 7, & 8 are correct
d. 1, 3, 4, 5, 6, & 7 are correct
e. 1, 3, 4, 6, 7, & 9 are correct

53. One can acquire a sense of power in three ways. Which of the following is NOT one of them?

a. doing
b. being
c. controlling
d. inheriting

54. Power can be experienced on three levels. Which of the following is NOT one of those levels?

a. internally
b. personally
c. interactively
d. societally

55. Evaluate the following statements with regards to the effects of a sense of powerlessness on the part of inmates.

1. causes frustration
2. causes dissatisfaction
3. causes elation
4. causes pain
5. has a strong effect on officer/inmate relations

a. all of the above statements are true
b. statements 1, 2, 3 & 5 are true
c. statements 2, 3, 4 & 4 are true
d. statements 1, 3, 4 & 5 are true
e. statements 1, 2, 4 & 5 are true

56. The bases of discretion include which of the following items?

a. intelligence
b. education
c. experience
d. all of the above
e. only a & b above

57. List the six stages of the cultural effectiveness continuum.

1.

2.

3.

4.

5.

6.

58. Evaluate the following statements with regards to "cultural destructiveness."

1. It is the most negative end of continuum.
2. It assumes that the dominant culture is superior.
3. Other cultures should be destroyed, exploited, or removed.
4. It assumes that the dominant culture is inferior.

a. statements 1, 2, & 4 are true
b. statements 1, 3, & 4 are true
c. statements 2, 3, & 4 are true
d. statements 1, 2, & 3 are true
e. only statements 2 & 3 are true

59. Which of the following gives the best definition for the term "mental disorder?"

a. any psychosis, neurosis, or psychopathology that produces socially acceptable behavior
b. persons who have significantly subaverage intelligence and generally lack the abilities to meet standards of personal independence and social responsibility expected of their age, cultural group, and community
c. psychological and/or behavioral problems which impair functioning in daily living
d. persons who do not suffer from an impairment of the emotional processes, of the ability to exercise conscious control of one's actions, or of the ability to perceive reality or to understand
e. any medical condition that results in a physical or emotional disability

60. Which of the following is NOT considered to be a mental disorder?

a. mental retardation
b. developmental disability
c. intoxication
d. drug addiction
e. none of the above are mental disorders

61. Which of the following refers to a disturbance in feelings or emotions, such as depression?

a. thought disorder
b. mood disorder
c. personality disorder
d. organic disorder
e. none of the above

62. Hearing voices which are not present and seeing people or things that are not present describes which of the following terms?

a. hallucinations
b. intense anxiety
c. paranoia
d. delusions
e. depression

63. Which of the following is NOT a symptom of mental illness?

a. delayed gratification
b. hallucinations
c. intense anxiety
d. talking to oneself
e. paranoia

64. What basic procedures should an officer follow when dealing with a mentally ill person?

a. try to calm the person down
b. take as much time as necessary and do not hurry
c. try to provoke the person so you can justify the need to restrain him or her
d. threaten to hurt the person so he or she will retreat and forget about where the backup officer is
e. a & b above

65. Signs and symptoms which might be observed when dealing with a person with mental disorders could include which of the following?

a. hallucinations
b. paranoia
c. delusions
d. all of the above
e. b & c above

66. Evaluate the following statements:

1. An inmate may be admitted to a mental health treatment facility if he or she is mentally ill and is in need of care and treatment.

2. An inmate who is being admitted to a mental health treatment facility has the right to proper notice and a hearing in the local county court.

3. An inmate who is admitted to a mental health treatment facility is entitled to a court review after six months.

a. all three statements are true
b. only statements 1 & 2 are true
c. only statements 1 & 3 are true
d. only statements 2 & 3 are true
e. all three statements are false

67. Which of the following gives the best definition for the term "mental retardation?"

a. persons who suffer from an impairment of the emotional processes, of the ability to exercise conscious control of one's actions, or of the ability to perceive reality or to understand
b. persons suffering from a fundamental mental derangement characterized by defective or lost contact with reality
c. persons who have significantly subaverage intelligence and generally lack the abilities to meet standards of personal independence and social responsibility expected of their age, cultural group, and community
d. any psychosis, neurosis, or psychopathology that produces anti-social behavior
e. any medical condition that results in a physical or emotional disability

68. Mental retardation may be caused by which of the following?

a. trauma to the brain due to severe head injury
b. genetic abnormalities
c. prenatal injuries
d. illnesses, such as encephalitis or meningitis
e. all of the above

69. Evaluate the following statements:

1. Persons who are mentally retarded are usually more violent than the general population.

2. Generally, people with mental retardation have abnormal physical characteristics and immediately demonstrate characteristics of mental retardation.

3. Mental retardation is a disability that lasts a lifetime and can never be cured.

a. all three statements are false
b. only statements 1 & 2 are false
c. only statements 1 & 3 are false
d. only statements 2 & 3 are false
e. all three statements are true

70. A mentally retarded person may:

a. need additional time to answer questions
b. be easily intimidated
c. be eager to please
d. be easily manipulated by other inmates
e. all of the above

71. The majority of persons identified as being mentally retarded are classified in which of the following groups?

a. severely retarded
b. moderately retarded
c. mildly retarded
d. no visible signs
e. clinically depressed

72. Evaluate the following statements:

1. People with mental retardation may need additional time to respond to questions.

2. People with mental retardation may be unable to remember instructions or rules.

3. A person who is mentally retarded may be coerced by other inmates to break rules.

a. all three statements are false
b. only statements 1 & 2 are true
c. only statements 1 & 3 are true
d. only statements 2 & 3 are true
e. all three statements are true

73. A person who asks a corrections officer to repeat himself or herself several times during the course of a conversation may be exhibiting what type of an impairment?

a. understanding
b. hearing
c. visual
d. tactile
e. mental

74. Evaluate the following statements:

1. There have been instances where canes, crutches, and prostheses have been used to transport contraband.

2. A suspect who is deaf has the right to a professional interpreter during any interrogation.

3. The Department of Corrections has a coordinator who can assist with appropriate placement and arrangements for physically handicapped inmates.

a. all three statements are false
b. only statements 1 & 2 are true
c. only statements 1 & 3 are true
d. only statements 2 & 3 are true
e. all three statements are true

75. Evaluate the following statements:

1. In dealing with a deaf individual, the officer should remember that lip reading is the most reliable method of communication.

2. Stairways, curbs, and narrow doors are some architectural barriers that people with mobility impairments sometimes face.

3. A deaf suspect does not have the legal right to a professional interpreter, but he or she does have the legal right to make a phone call using a telecommunication device (TDD) for the deaf.

a. all three statements are false
b. only statements 1 & 2 are false
c. only statements 1 & 3 are false
d. only statements 2 & 3 are false
e. all three statements are true

76. Which of the following could be considered auxiliary means of communication?

a. sign language
b. writing
c. lip reading
d. all of the above
e. a & c above only

77. Which of the following is the best way for an officer to assist the mobility of a visually-impaired individual?

a. grab the individual's clothing in the back and lead him or her
b. gently push the individual ahead of you in the right direction
c. ask the individual to take your arm
d. talk to the person so he or she can follow the sound of your voice
e. none of the above

78. Substance abuse is best defined by which of the following?

a. physical and/or psychological dependence on a substance

b. continual or frequent use of a substance
c. the use of a substance which alters mental or physical functioning, whether use is legal, illegal, therapeutic, or recreational
d. the use of a substance, unintentionally or inappropriately, in excess of its intended amount or purpose which often results in the impaired well-being of the user
e. continued use of a substance despite the knowledge that the substance causes or worsens a recurring or persistent social, occupational, psychological, or physical problem; or repeated use of the substance in situations when its use is physically hazardous

79. A physical and/or psychological dependence on a substance characterized by withdrawal symptoms is the definition for which of the following terms?

a. tolerance
b. addiction
c. habituation
d. physical dependence
e. psychological dependence

80. Which of the following terms refers to a physical resistance to a substance's effects so that larger amounts are required to produce the desired effect?

a. addiction
b. habituation
c. withdrawal
d. tolerance
e. detoxification

81. What is the condition called when substances change the user's body system so that the body becomes accustomed to and needs the substance to function normally?

a. physical dependence
b. psychological dependence
c. withdrawal
d. detoxification
e. habituation

82. Which of the following terms refers to the condition that exists when substances change the user's mental condition so that it becomes difficult to control or stop use because the user believes the substance is necessary to feel good or normal?

a. detoxification
b. psychological dependence
c. physical dependence
d. tolerance
e. habituation

83. The process by which a person who is physically or psychologically dependent on a substance is brought to a substance-free state is known as what?

a. habituation
b. tolerance
c. detoxification
d. addiction
e. withdrawal

84. An individual who has an overpowering need or compulsion to continue taking a drug and to obtain it by any means, has a tendency to increase the dosage, has a physical as well as psychological dependence on the drug, and suffers detrimental effects is suffering from which of the following?

a. physical dependence
b. drug habituation
c. drug addiction
d. withdrawal
e. detoxification

85. Evaluate the following statements:

1. Factors which can influence a drug's effects on a user would include the user's expectations, physical state, tolerance of the user, and the potency of drug.

2. While a number of factors can influence drug effects on an individual, the user's reason for using a drug should have no effect.

3. Substance abusers do not pose a higher than normal suicide risk.

a. all three statements are false
b. only statements 1 & 2 are false
c. only statements 1 & 3 are false
d. only statements 2 & 3 are false
e. all three statements are true

86. Which of the following are often associated with substance abuse?

a. drug-related emergencies such as overdoses or toxic reactions

b. criminal acts, family and job problems, good health
c. poor health, criminal acts, loss of control
d. all of the above
e. a & c above only

87. About how long does it usually take before drugs that are injected have an effect?

a. immediately
b. within 2 minutes or less
c. approximately 10 minutes
d. delayed 20 minutes or more

88. About how long does it usually take before drugs that are inhaled have an effect?

a. immediately
b. in about 2 minutes
c. delayed 20 minutes or more
d. in about 10 minutes
e. c or d above could be correct, depending on the type of drug

89. About how long does it usually take before drugs that are ingested have an effect?

a. immediately
b. about 2 minutes or less
c. delayed 20 minutes or more
d. about 10 minutes or less
e. varies according to the type of drug

90. An individual under the influence of, or withdrawing from, drugs or alcohol might display which of the following signs?

a. a change in breathing patterns
b. nausea, vomiting
c. a blank, blood-shot, glassy-eyed appearance
d. tremors or convulsions
e. all of the above

91. A person is generally considered to be in danger or becoming comatose, and possibly even dying, if his or her blood alcohol content exceeds which level?

a. .10%
b. .15%
c. .20%
d. .30%
e. .40%

92. Symptoms of different illnesses may sometimes resemble drunkenness. Which of the following is NOT one of those sicknesses?

a. diabetic shock
b. smallpox
c. carbon monoxide poisoning
d. stroke
e. head injury

93. Which of the following items is NOT a common crisis situation in a correctional facility society?

a. divorce or other family problems due to imprisonment
b. news concerning the loss of a loved one
c. receiving a college scholarship
d. a significant disciplinary infraction
e. a recommended transfer that is perceived as adverse

94. What is the stage of a crisis called in which there are few observable symptoms even though the crisis-producing dynamics are present?

a. symptomatic level
b. crucial level
c. pre-symptomatic level
d. post-crisis level
e. acute level

95. What is the common state of crisis called in which the person has mostly lost control?

a. pre-symptomatic level
b. symptomatic level
c. crucial level
d. acute level
e. post-crisis level

96. Which of the following is NOT a common phase of an emotional response to a crisis?

a. high anxiety
b. grief
c. gloating
d. anger
e. remorse

97. Which of the below is NOT a step of crisis intervention?

a. arrest
b. assessment
c. decision point

d. referral
e. none of the above

98. Which of the following statements is NOT a recommended procedure for handling crisis situations?
    a. asking the individual questions to collect information about the problem
    b. using force only to the degree necessary to gain control
    c. asking the person in crisis for suggestions to resolve the crisis
    d. making a promise to the individual even though you know you cannot keep it
    e. using calming techniques to defuse a volatile situation

99. Which of the following is NOT a calming technique that could be useful in a crisis situation?
    a. yelling and shouting to make a point
    b. speaking in a calm and confident voice
    c. trying to get the person(s) to sit down
    d. respecting the individual's personal space
    e. treat the situation in a professional manner

100. Which of the following actions has the potential to result in high arousal during a crisis situation?
    a. physical contact
    b. profane or derogatory language
    c. derogatory comments
    d. interrupting a disputant who is talking
    e. all of the above

101. What is the body's preparation when threatened to either stand and fight or run away called?
    a. stress
    b. fight or flight response
    c. stressor
    d. stimuli
    e. eustress

102. Which of the following is NOT a recognized category of potential stressors?
    a. environmental
    b. global
    c. personal
    d. work-related
    e. self-induced

103. Poor supervision would be an example of which category of stress for corrections officers?
    a. environmental
    b. personal
    c. self-induced
    d. work-related
    e. internal

104. Which of the following work-related stressors is NOT internal to the correctional organization?
    a. poor training
    b. shift work
    c. inadequate pay
    d. negative stories in the media
    e. inadequate manpower allocation

105. Which of the following refers to any stress associated with pleasant experiences or positive emotions?
    a. chronic stressors
    b. distress
    c. eustress
    d. exhaustion
    e. adaptation

106. Which of the following items references the stages in the General Adaptation Syndrome?
    a. alarm, resistance, exhaustion
    b. alarm, fight-or-flight, exhaustion
    c. observation, alarm, exhaustion
    d. observation, exposure, reaction
    e. alarm, recovery, retrenchment

107. Evaluate the following statements:

    1. Long-term conditions that indirectly cause the stress reaction are known as chronic stressors.

    2. In the exhaustion stage of stress, the body attempts to adjust to the continued stressor and repair any damage.

    3. An increase in headaches, eating, and drinking are signs of immediate stress responses.

    a. all three statements are true
    b. only statements 1 & 2 are true
    c. only statements 1 & 3 are true
    d. only statements 2 & 3 are true
    e. all three statements are false

108. Which of the following items is intended to reduce stress?

a. physical exercise
b. relaxation
c. proper diet
d. improved mental health
e. all of the above

109. What is the name for the stage during stress reaction when the human body attempts to adjust to the continued stressor and repair damage or brings the effects of the stressor within tolerable limits?

a. alarm reaction stage
b. critical stage
c. exhaustion stage
d. resistance stage
e. repository stage

110. Which of the following can result from stress?

a. increased blood pressure
b. "flying off the handle"
c. ulcers
d. divorce
e. all of the above

111. What are the warning signs of stress for a corrections officer?

a. increased use of sick time
b. excessive use of alcohol
c. fatigue
d. excessive complaints regarding job performance
e. all of the above

112. Which of the following terms refers to long-term persistent conditions or situations that indirectly cause stress reaction?

a. episodic stressors
b. chronic stressors
c. eustress
d. exhaustion
e. nonepisodic alleviators

113. Which of the following would NOT be a recommended method of stress reduction?

a. temporary decompression with legal drugs or alcohol
b. physical exercise, especially aerobic events
c. proper diet and sleep patterns
d. meditation, biofeedback, self-hypnosis
e. vacations

114. High officer stress levels can have an impact on the organization. Which of the following is NOT one of those outcomes?

a. employee turnover
b. increased number of lawsuits
c. higher worker compensation costs
d. more use of officer sick time
e. all of the above

115. Which statement is NOT true about suicide?

a. people who talk about suicide do not end up killing themselves
b. most people consider suicide at some point in their lives
c. people who are depressed do not kill themselves
d. the suicide rate among teenagers has tripled in the last ten years
e. there is a higher incidence of suicidal behavior in correctional facilities than in any other setting

116. Accidents are the leading cause of death among young people. What is the second leading cause of death among youth?

a. homicide
b. suicide
c. drug overdose
d. child birth complications
e. AIDS

117. Evaluate the following statements:

1. Inmate populations consist of a high proportion of persons at suicide risk.

2. The correctional environment is conducive to suicidal behavior because it isolates inmates from significant others, causes shame, and it dehumanizes inmates.

3. One suicide in a correctional facility is often followed by a rash of suicides or attempted suicides.

a. all three statements are true.
b. only statements 1 & 2 are true.
c. only statements 1 & 3 are true.
d. only statements 2 & 3 are true.
e. all three statements are false.

118. Evaluate the following statements:

1. Over half the suicides occur within 12 hours of incarceration.

2. Younger inmates are more prone to suicide.

3. If a person makes threats to commit suicide, he or she probably is not serious about it.

a. all three statements are true.
b. only statements 1 & 2 are true.
c. only statements 1 & 3 are true.
d. only statements 2 & 3 are true.
e. all three statements are false.

119. When a person has difficulty sleeping, cries for no apparent reason, and is slow thinking, what mental condition is most likely to be present?

a. neurosis
b. paranoia
c. psychosis
d. depression
e. anemia

120. Which of the following may be warning signals of depression?

a. sleep difficulties
b. sitting in a fetal position
c. becomes agitated easily
d. all of the above
e. a & b above only

121. Which of the following events can trigger a crisis situation for an inmate?

a. sexual assault
b. death of a family member
c. parole denial
d. visitation
e. all of the above

122. Which of the following steps should a corrections officer take after arriving at a threatened suicide call?

a. start a conversation with the inmate
b. challenge the inmate to carry out the threat to see whether he or she is serious
c. preserve the scene in the event that a suicide does occur later
d. wait for back up and simply observe the inmate from behind cover
e. write a preliminary report

123. Evaluate the following statements:

1. One of the reasons someone may attempt suicide is to rejoin loved ones who have died.

2. If someone tells you that he or she wants to commit suicide, one way to test the person's intentions is to challenge him or her to do it.

3. One thing responding officers should do is remove onlookers or potentially disruptive persons from the scene.

a. all three statements are true
b. only statements 1 & 2 are true
c. only statements 1 & 3 are true
d. only statements 2 & 3 are true
e. all three statements are false

124. Evaluate the following statements:

1. When an inmate has attempted suicide, corrections officers should presume that the victim is alive until he or she is pronounced dead by a medical authority.

2. Only mentally ill inmates will attempt to commit suicide.

3. Placing a suicidal inmate in isolation is the only remedy available to corrections officers.

a. all three statements are false
b. only statements 1 & 2 are false
c. only statements 1 & 3 are false
d. only statements 2 & 3 are false
e. all three statements are true

Chapter 3 Answer Key

1. B
2. E
3. E
4. D
5. A
6. C
7. D
8. E
9. B
10. B

11. E
12. C
13. D
14. B
15. B
16. B
17. E
18. D
19. E
20. A

21. A
22. B
23. A
24. B
25. A
26. D
27. C
28. E
29. D
30. *

31. B
32. D
33. C
34. C
35. B
36. E
37. C
38. A
39. D
40. B

41. E
42. B
43. A
44. B
45. D
46. A
47. B
48. A
49. B
50. D

51. E
52. B
53. D
54. A
55. E
56. D
57. *
58. D
59. C
60. E

61. B
62. A
63. A
64. E
65. D
66. A
67. C
68. E
69. B
70. E

71. C
72. E
73. B
74. E
75. C
76. D
77. C
78. E
79. B
80. D

81. A
82. B
83. C
84. C
85. D
86. E
87. B
88. A
89. C
90. E

91. E
92. B
93. C
94. C
95. D
96. C
97. A
98. D
99. A
100. E

101. B
102. B
103. D
104. D
105. C
106. A
107. C
108. E
109. D
110. E

111. E
112. B
113. A
114. E
115. A
116. B
117. A
118. B
119. D
120. D
121. E
122. A
123. C
124. D

Answers to List Questions

30.
(1) understand but do not use the dialect
(2) use proper names
(3) exercise genuineness
(4) avoid game-playing and psychological ploys
(5) acknowledge racial and ethnic issues nondefensively
(6) permit and accept expressive behaviors
(7) avoid presenting yourself as "the system"

57.
(1) cultural proficiency
(2) cultural effectiveness
(3) cultural pre-effectiveness
(4) cultural blindness
(5) cultural incapacity
(6) cultural destructiveness

CHAPTER 4

CORRECTIONAL OPERATIONS

Chapter Overview

This portion of your preparation for the Florida Corrections Officer Certification Examination focuses upon various operational and legal procedures, as well as state rules and regulations, with which officers must be familiar. Just as in earlier chapters of this guide, the questions that appear here were chosen to reflect the goals and objectives that guide the police academy training.

By the time you complete this section, you should have a firm understanding of the following topics:

- Chain of Command and Organization
- Inspection Services
- Facility Inspection Techniques
- Vehicle Inspection Techniques
- Safety Requirements and Procedures
- Environmental Health Requirements and Procedures
- Health Care Service Requirements and Procedures
- Food Service Requirements and Procedures
- Control Room Operations and Procedures
- Intake Procedures
- Inmate Property Control Procedures
- Classification Procedures
- Fingerprinting
- Transfer Procedures
- Release Procedures
- Bonding Procedures
- Recognition, Control, and Disposal of Contraband
- Disciplinary Procedures
- Confinement Procedures
- Referral Procedures
- Cell and Area Search Techniques
- Officer Survival Considerations
- Patrol Concepts and Techniques
- Patrol Hazards
- Visual Perception/Discrimination and Observation Techniques
- Tool and Sensitive Item Control Concepts and Procedures
- Key Control Concepts and Procedures
- Accountability Concepts and Procedures
- Security Equipment
- Inmate Movement Requirements and Procedures
- Preliminary and Follow-Up Investigation Procedures
- Crime Scene Search Procedures
- Evidence Handling Procedures
- Chain of Custody Concepts
- State Rules and Regulations
- Prisoner Transport Methods

Questions

1. Evaluate the following statements:

   1. "Chain of command" can be defined as that connection or linkage of authority and responsibility that joins one level of an organization to another.

   2. "Chain of command" can be defined as that connection or linkage of communications and responsibility that joins together several departments of the same level in an organization.

   3. "Organization" can be defined as a group of two or more people who cooperate to accomplish an objective or a set of objectives.

   a. all three statements are true
   b. only statements 1 & 2 are true
   c. only statements 1 & 3 are true
   d. only statements 2 & 3 are true
   e. all three statements are false

2. Evaluate the following statements:

   1. The purpose of organization and chain of command is to limit the number of people who report to the chief executive officer, thereby allowing a "democratic" organization.

   2. The purpose of organization and chain of command is to provide a uniform channeling of information, authority, and responsibility throughout the organizational structure.

   3. The purpose of organization and chain of command is to facilitate the accomplishment of objectives and to provide a structural relationship between each employee and the chief executive officer.

   a. all three statements are true
   b. only statements 1 & 2 are true
   c. only statements 1 & 3 are true
   d. only statements 2 & 3 are true
   e. all three statements are false

3. Which of the following terms refers to a group of two or more people who cooperate in order to accomplish an objective?

   a. chain of command
   b. organization
   c. conspiracy
   d. policy mandate
   e. none of the above

4. Evaluate the following statements:

   1. Important considerations for effective organization would include achievement of a single purpose and the coordination of activities, not people.

   2. Important considerations for effective organization would include ensuring that each person comprehends the extent of his or her duties and identifying each task as the unmistakable duty of a particular person.

   3. An important consideration for effective organization is the ability to remain inflexible in the face of change.

   a. all three statements are true
   b. only statements 1 & 2 are true
   c. only statements 1 & 3 are true
   d. only statements 2 & 3 are true
   e. all three statements are false

5. Which of the following terms means checking to see that equipment, facilities, and people meet a standard?

   a. search
   b. seizure
   c. official mandate
   d. inspection
   e. none of the above

6. Which of the following categories of official personnel conduct inspections in Florida prisons?

   a. officers, supervisors, managers
   b. prison inspectors and state fire inspectors
   c. assistant attorneys and general attorneys
   d. all of the above
   e. a & b above only

7. Evaluate the following statements:

   1. The elements of safe prisoner transport include establishing clear and comprehensive agency guidelines, adhering to these guidelines, and making sure that an adequate number of personnel are available.

   2. One element of safe prisoner transport is to make sure that seat belts are removed from prisoners' seats.

   3. One officer should check the transport vehicle to see that it is properly equipped and in good

working order prior to conducting the transport.

a. all three statements are true
b. only statements 1 & 2 are true
c. only statements 1 & 3 are true
d. only statements 2 & 3 are true
e. all three statements are false

8. Why conduct inspections?

a. provide for the safety of inmates, staff, and visitors
b. maintain healthy conditions within the facility
c. provide and ensure the proper organization of the facility
d. all of the above
e. a & b above only

9. Prisoners are searched and restrained prior to transport to:

a. prevent escapes
b. confiscate any weapons or contraband
c. ensure officer safety
d. all of the above
e. a & c above only

10. A basic mistake when conducting prisoner transports is to:

a. make assumptions of a prisoner's potential threat based on appearance
b. use the seriousness of a prisoner's crime as an indicator of potential threat
c. use additional precautionary procedures when transporting juveniles, injured persons, or members of the opposite sex
d. all of the above
e. a & b above only

11. Facility inspection should be performed:

a. routinely on a regular schedule
b. before and after any activity or when a problem is suspected
c. randomly and never on a regular schedule
d. both a & b are correct
e. both b & c are correct

12. Prison inspectors are responsible for checking all of the following EXCEPT:

a. orderliness
b. cleanliness of facility
c. comfort of facility
d. method and manner that food is served
e. b & c above only

13. Evaluate the following statements:

1. Officers should be familiar with agency standards and consult the agency's inspection guidelines for each type of inspection.

2. Officers should leave inmates in the area under inspection, search the inmates, and then place the inmates under supervision while the inspection is conducted.

3. Officers should review safety procedures for inspecting operation of equipment and consult inventory or identification lists.

a. all three statements are true
b. only statements 1 & 2 are true
c. only statements 1 & 3 are true
d. only statements 2 & 3 are true
e. all three statements are false

14. Inspection results should be:

a. entered in the officer's personal notebook so that a record is available upon request
b. entered in the appropriate log or report form and submitted to a supervisor
c. immediately reported to supervisor if any dangerous situations are noted
d. all of the above
e. b & c above only

15. Evaluate the following statements:

1. Unsanitary facilities constitute cruel and unusual punishment, a violation of the Eighth Amendment.

2. Inmates are responsible for the environmental health program in a correctional institution.

3. Inmates have the right to clean, orderly, and safe surroundings

a. all three statements are true
b. only statements 1 & 2 are true
c. only statements 1 & 3 are true
d. only statements 2 & 3 are true
e. all three statements are false

16. Evaluate the following statements:

1. The duties of a prison inspector include inspecting the general conditions of each facility.

2. The duties of a prison inspector include inspecting the number and condition of prisoners.

3. The duties of a prison inspector include inspecting the psychological conditions at a facility.

a. all three statements are true
b. only statements 1 & 2 are true
c. only statements 1 & 3 are true
d. only statements 2 & 3 are true
e. all three statements are false

17. Inspections should be performed in all areas EXCEPT:

a. visitation areas
b. administrative areas
c. dining halls
d. cells
e. dorms

18. Areas of safety concern within a correctional facility or setting include:

a. housing, work crews, recreational areas
b. confinement, work crews, recreational areas
c. housing, administration, work crews
d. work crews, administration, dining area
e. parking lots and access roads

19. Potential hazards to be considered while supervising work crews would include:

a. proper lifting techniques and improper use of tools
b. proper driving techniques and failure to wear safety equipment
c. improper use of tools and proper driving techniques
d. failure to wear safety equipment and improper use of tools
e. none of the above

20. Evaluate the following statements:

1. Inmates have the right to clean, orderly, and safe surroundings.

2. Unsanitary facilities constitute cruel and unusual punishment; a violation of the Eight Amendment.

3. Inmates have the right to have access to television, radio, and cable-TV programs in their cells.

a. all three statements are true
b. only statements 1 & 2 are true
c. only statements 1 & 3 are true
d. only statements 2 & 3 are true
e. all three statements are false

21. Responsibility for the environmental health program in a correctional facility resides with whom?

a. supervisors
b. officers
c. staff
d. management
e. inmates

22. When delousing an inmate, a correctional officer would be expected to:

a. direct inmate to the shower and help the inmate undress
b. issue medicated soap
c. issue clean institutional clothing to inmate
d. all of the above
e. b & c above only

23. Evaluate the following statements:

1. Implied consent from a parent or guardian is required before administering any type of medical treatment to juveniles.

2. Each inmate should have access to quality services that meets professional standards.

3. Inmates should expect to receive their medical treatment in a private setting with consideration for the patient's dignity and feelings.

a. all three statements are true
b. only statements 1 & 2 are true
c. only statements 1 & 3 are true
d. only statements 2 & 3 are true
e. all three statements are false

24. The functions of health care services within an institution include which of the following?

a. conducting strip searches of inmates upon intake
b. making written policies and procedures available to inmates concerning services
c. performing medical screening upon intake
d. all of the above
e. b & c above only

25. One function of health care services is to provide dental screening, hygiene, examination, and treatment.

a. true
b. false

26. With regard to health care, a correctional officer is expected to:

a. perform first responder techniques if necessary
b. distribute special diets to inmates as directed by medical personnel
c. supervise delousing procedures
d. all of the above
e. a & c above only

27. Procedures to follow when an inmate is suspected or confirmed to have a communicable disease include all of the following EXCEPT which one?

a. arrange for medical attention
b. remove individual from general population
c. place in an area with minimal ventilation
d. house in isolation area
e. observe closely and record progress accurately

28. Evaluate the following statements:

1. An inmate has the right to three meals per day, at least two of these meals being hot.

2. An inmate has the right to breakfast never more than 14 hours following the beginning of the evening meal.

3. Food can never be withheld as punishment or given as a reward.

a. all three statements are true
b. only statements 1 & 2 are true
c. only statements 1 & 3 are true
d. only statements 2 & 3 are true
e. all three statements are false

29. Evaluate the following statements:

1. Food service is the subject of many lawsuits.

2. Poor food is a major cause of prison riots.

3. Improper food service seldom influences jail or institution climate.

a. all three statements are true
b. only statements 1 & 2 are true
c. only statements 1 & 3 are true
d. only statements 2 & 3 are true
e. all three statements are false

30. Inmates have the right to a special diet if it is a religious preference.

a. true
b. false

31. The duties of a correctional officer with regard to the food service program include:

a. supervision of inmates preparing and serving food
b. maintaining order during meals
c. accounting for trays, silverware, utensils, equipment, and left-over food at the end of the meal
d. all of the above
e. b & c above only

32. Special security considerations in the food service program would include:

a. strict accounting of silverware that could be fashioned into weapons
b. a small number of inmates congregated in one area could be the start of a potential disturbance
c. possibility of contraband transmitted in food supplies
d. all of the above
e. a & c above only

33. Evaluate the following statements:

1. Use of tobacco, smoking, or spitting near food is allowed only before and after inmates have been served.

2. All food service workers are required to take a physical exam within 30 days after entry into food service.

3. Hot foods must reach 112 degrees Fahrenheit.

a. all three statements are true
b. only statements 1 & 2 are true
c. only statements 1 & 3 are true
d. only statements 2 & 3 are true
e. all three statements are false

34. Evaluate the following statements:

1. Utensils used in the food service program are to be sterilized at 180 degrees F.

2. Poisons and toxins may be stored in cabinets with food items only if the cabinet is under lock and key.

3. Refrigerated foods should be stored at -35 to -40 degrees F.

a. all three statements are true
b. only statements 1 & 2 are true
c. only statements 1 & 3 are true
d. only statements 2 & 3 are true
e. all three statements are false

35. What is the appropriate freezer temperature for food storage?

a. -40 degrees or less
b. -30 degrees or less
c. -20 degrees or less
d. -10 degrees or less
e. 0 degrees or less

36. The general purposes of the control center or control room are:

a. to function as the nerve center of a facility
b. to integrate all external and internal security and communication networks
c. to control access to and from the facility and within the facility
d. all of the above
e. a & b above only

37. Evaluate the following statements with regard to the control center.

1. Typical tasks of control center personnel include issuing weapons, ammunition, restraints, and riot control equipment on the order of shift supervisor

2. Typical tasks of control center personnel include counting and maintaining the inmate status board.

3. Control center personnel should maintain a list of inmate telephone numbers and next of kin and their telephone numbers.

a. all three statements are true
b. only statements 1 & 2 are true
c. only statements 1 & 3 are true
d. only statements 2 & 3 are true
e. all three statements are false

38. A typical task of control center personnel would be to control lighting and power as needed.

a. true
b. false

39. Maintaining information on inmate lock-ups, releases, or movements is NOT a task or responsibility for control center personnel.

a. true
b. false

40. Which of the following should be recorded on control center logs?

1. institutional counts
2. escape or escape attempt information
3. fog or weather reports
4. vehicle or equipment breakdowns
5. inmates received and/or discharged

a. all should be recorded
b. 1, 2, and 4 should be recorded
c. 1, 2, 3, and 4 should be recorded
d. 1, 2, 4, and 5 should be recorded
e. 2, 3, 4, and 5 should be recorded

41. Evaluate the following statements:

1. The control center must be staffed 24 hours per day, five days per week.

2. Control center staff function as decision-makers.

3. Only correctional employees or inmates on trustee status should perform cleaning duties in control center.

a. all three statements are true
b. only statements 1 & 2 are true
c. only statements 1 & 3 are true
d. only statements 2 & 3 are true
e. all three statements are false

42. Which of the following is NOT a special problem associated with the intake process?

a. may be a traumatic situation for an inmate
b. the potential for danger for either the inmate or the correctional officer is almost nonexistent because the setting is new to the inmate
c. high anxiety can be manifested by physical resistance and violence
d. many emergency situations occur during intake process
e. b & c above only

43. A complete and successful intake program would accomplish which of the following?

a. reduce anxiety levels for newly committed inmates

b. ensure complete medical and dental health screenings
c. issue clothing and personal toiletry items
d. all of the above
e. a & c above only

44. Evaluate the following statements:

1. The intake officer should examine the credentials of the escorting officer and receive commitment orders from him or her.

2. The intake officer should advise incoming inmates to go to personnel the following day to receive clothing and personal hygiene items.

3. The intake officer should advise an incoming inmate about the procedure for making an appointment with the shift supervisor in order to obtain phone privileges.

a. all three statements are true
b. only statement 1 is true
c. only statements 1 & 3 are true
d. only statement 3 is true
e. all three statements are false

45. A file should be maintained on each inmate which would include documentation of:

a. record of any detainer
b. fingerprint card
c. date of release and a current photograph
d. all of the above
e. a & c above only

46. While medical and dental information should be maintained in an inmate's file, psychological information should not be placed in the file because this information is considered privileged and should not be disclosed.

a. true
b. false

47. Important considerations with regard to the intake process include which of the following?

a. provide lockers in the security perimeter so that escorting officers may secure their weapons
b. the officer responsible for processing should be of same gender as the inmate being admitted
c. admit juveniles only for processing
d. all of the above
e. a & b above only

48. Officers involved in the intake process should use frisk search procedures for unsentenced persons charged with minor offenses but should strip search others.

a. true
b. false

49. Which of the following options can be used during the intake process to dispose of an inmate's personal property?

a. return to inmate to be retained in his or her possession
b. return to home or family address
c. deposit money in inmate account
d. all of the above
e. b & c above only

50. Items of personal property which may be retained in an inmate's possession would include which of the following?

a. legal documents, prescription glasses, address book or list, family pictures
b. legal documents, sunglasses, address book or list, prescription glasses
c. legal documents, prescription glasses, common pocket knife, address book or list
d. all of the above
e. a & b above only

51. Evaluate the following statements:

1. When preparing a property inventory list/receipt, the officer should write an accurate description of all property by appearance.

2. When preparing a property inventory list/receipt, the officer should list all currency by serial number and all credit cards by number.

3. When preparing a property inventory list/receipt, the officer should count each item and enter the appropriate quantity.

a. all three statements are true
b. only statements 1 & 2 are true
c. only statements 1 & 3 are true
d. only statements 2 & 3 are true
e. all three statements are false

52. Evaluate the following statements:

1. When depositing an inmate's money, the correctional officer should count the money while the inmate watches.

2. When depositing an inmate's money, the correctional officer should have the inmate review the receipt for accuracy.

3. When depositing an inmate's money, the correctional should have the inmate sign to verify the accuracy of receipt.

a. all three statements are true
b. only statements 1 & 2 are true
c. only statements 2 & 3 are true
d. only statements 1 & 3 are true
e. all three statements are false

53. Evaluate the following statements:

1. Any medicines possessed by inmate upon intake should be turned over to medical personnel with the appropriate notation made on the inmate's record.

2. An inmate must give written authorization before a correctional officer can release any of the inmate's personal property to family or friends.

3. If an inmate is transferred to another facility, his or her personal property should be transported with him or her in a sealed container.

a. all three statements are true
b. only statements 1 & 2 are true
c. only statements 2 & 3 are true
d. only statements 1 & 3 are true
e. all three statements are false

54. "The systematic grouping of inmates into categories based on shared characteristics and/or behavioral patterns to ensure the safety and security of the individual inmate as well as the smooth operation of the facility" is the definition for which of the following terms?

a. facilitation
b. categorization
c. classification
d. grouping
e. distribution

55. The importance of a well-defined and correctly implemented inmate classification system includes which of the following?

a. ensures public safety by correctly determining necessary custody levels
b. ensures safety and security of the individual inmate
c. provides for a cost-effective operation
d. all of the above
e. b & c above only

56. Evaluate the following statements:

1. Male prisoners should be segregated from female prisoners in county and municipal facilities.

2. Pretrial detainees should be segregated from convicted inmates in county and municipal facilities.

3. Nonviolent inmates should be segregated from violent inmates in county and municipal facilities.

a. all three statements are true
b. only statements 1 & 2 are true
c. only statements 2 & 3 are true
d. only statements 1 & 3 are true
e. all three statements are false

57. Evaluate the following statements:

1. Special needs inmates should be segregated from the general population.

2. Adults should be separated from juveniles.

3. Old inmates should be segregated from the general population.

a. all three statements are true
b. only statements 1 & 2 are true
c. only statements 2 & 3 are true
d. only statements 1 & 3 are true
e. all three statements are false

58. Which of the following is NOT a special needs inmate?

a. sexual deviate
b. an elderly person
c. emotionally disturbed
d. a racial minority member
e. b & c above only

59. Which of the following is NOT a recognized custody classification for inmates in state correctional facilities?

a. potential death row inmates
b. incorrigible inmates for whom a total lockup is required
c. inmates who have had difficulty in the system but who have not yet proven themselves incorrigible
d. inmates for whom there is some hope of rehabilitation

e. inmates for whom there is no hope of rehabilitation

60. Which of the following sources or types of information is NOT used in an inmate's initial classification?

a. investigative reports
b. medical and psychological screening
c. county jail report
d. birth certificate
e. arrest history

61. Which of the following topics would NOT be discussed during the inmate's classification interview?

a. family background and family unit
b. visitation procedures
c. the inmate's yearly earnings prior to commitment
d. the inmate's attitude about the sentence
e. b and c only

62. The criteria for placing inmates in an appropriate custody level include all of the following EXCEPT which one?

a. most appropriate housing assignment
b. degree of supervision and/or escort required
c. an inmate's request for liberal visitation criteria
d. access to programs and activities
e. c & d above only

63. Which of the following is NOT a criterion for assessing custody level and the degree of custody supervision?

a. any change in an inmate's legal status
b. request from the inmate's girlfriend or boyfriend
c. completion of inmate's program or assignment
d. change in sentence and release status
e. request from inmate himself or herself

64. Evaluate the following statements with regard to classification:

1. Segregating inmates on the basis of race, creed or national origin is a valid classification procedure.

2. Inmate reclassification evaluations should occur on a monthly basis.

3. The inmate should be present and be allowed to participate in the classification deliberations whenever possible.

a. all three statements are true
b. only statement 1 is true
c. only statement 2 is true
d. only statement 3 is true
e. all three statements are false

65. Why is it important to obtain clear and legible fingerprints from inmates?

a. to establish the Automated Fingerprint Identification System (AFIS)
b. to make an identification against existing records
c. to show professionalism
d. all of the above
e. a & b above only

66. To whom are inmate fingerprint cards/records routed?

a. FBI
b. FDLE
c. originating agency
d. all of the above
e. a & b above only

67. What are the two types of fingerprint impressions?

a. rolled and plain or simultaneous
b. rolled and palm
c. plain or simultaneous and palm
d. whorl and delta
e. ridges and lines

68. Different fingerprint cards are used to fingerprint persons who are a criminal, a juvenile, or a job applicant.

a. true
b. false

69. Which of the following is NOT a general procedure when fingerprinting somebody?

a. direct the subject to thoroughly wash and dry his or her hands
b. begin printing with subject's left little finger
c. direct the subject on proper stance
d. ink the finger to just below the first joint
e. apply pressure uniformly

70. Both the inmate who was fingerprinted and the correctional officer who fingerprinted the inmate should sign the fingerprint card upon completion.

a. true
b. false

71. What kind of an entry should an officer insert on the plain impressions area if the person being fingerprinted has an amputated finger?

a. N/A
b. UNK
c. amputated
d. none
e. simply leave the location blank

72. Which of the following are valid reasons for transferring inmates?

a. management or security reasons
b. on an emergency basis due to disturbances
c. to prevent or reduce inmate overcrowding
d. medical care
e. all of the above

73. Which of the following is NOT an appropriate procedure when transferring an inmate?

a. receive authorization for the transfer
b. transport the inmate's files or records
c. search the inmate prior to transport
d. make a positive identification of the inmate being transferred through pictures and fingerprints
e. let the inmate take physical custody of all property after he or she has signed an updated inventory list

74. Who is responsible for relaying a transferred inmate's institutional file, medical, dental, and psychological records to the receiving institution?

a. the inmate being transported
b. the U. S. Post Office via registered letter
c. the transporting officer
d. a correctional supervisor above the rank of Lieutenant
e. the sentencing court

75. Inmates can be released from a correctional facility in a number of different ways. Which of the following is NOT one of those mechanisms?

a. community control
b. bond
c. parole
d. expiration of sentence
e. pardon

76. Which of the following documentation is needed to authorize an inmate's release?

a. estreature of bond form
b. court order or writ
c. posting of bond or pretrial release form
d. a notarized letter from the victim stating that he or she is in agreement with the release
e. b & c above only

77. Which of the following items would NOT appear in an inmate's "release plan?"

a. the church to be attended, the pastor's name and phone number, denomination of church
b. address where the inmate will reside
c. employment possibilities, including the name, address, and type of work
d. special needs such as detoxification or drug counseling
e. party to whom restitution is owed and a payment schedule

78. A telephone call is received ordering the release of an inmate. What standard procedure should be followed in this instance?

a. check the work roster to determine whether the person who called in the release holds the rank of Sergeant or above
b. advise the person calling in the release to call you back five minutes later at a different phone number to be sure he is who he says he is
c. refuse to release the inmate until written orders are delivered
d. verify release authorization by making a return call to the person who called in the release
e. contact the sentencing judge to see whether the order is valid

79. Which of the following terms refers to a written agreement, usually involving a sum of money, wherein a person accused of a crime is released from custody pending trial and forfeits the sum of money if the agreement is violated?

a. pretrial release
b. duces tecum
c. parole
d. bond
e. released on one's own recognizance

80. Evaluate the following statements:

1. One advantage of releasing a person on bond is that many accused people lose their jobs while in custody awaiting a court hearing.

2. One advantage of releasing a person on bond is that the accused can support his or her family and earn money to pay for counsel of his or her choice.

3. One advantage of releasing a person on bond is that it reduces the financial burden on jails and helps to reduce jail overcrowding.

a. all three statements are true
b. only statements 1 & 2 are true
c. only statement 2 is true
d. only statements 2 & 3 are true
e. all three statements are false

81. Evaluate the following statements:

1. A disadvantage of releasing a person on bond is that the accused may flee the jurisdiction or commit other crimes.

2. A disadvantage of the bond system is that it typically denies release to rich people, but releases poor people.

3. The purpose of bond is to ensure that the accused will return to stand trial.

a. all three statements are true
b. only statements 1 & 2 are true
c. only statements 2 & 3 are true
d. only statements 1 & 3 are true
e. all three statements are false

82. Evaluate the following statements with regard to the legal rights of the accused.

1. The Eighth Amendment stipulates that an accused person has the right to reasonable bond. The Fourteenth Amendment makes bond binding on states.

2. The sole purpose of bond is to assure the victim's presence at trial.

3. Bond must be set in light of a person's community ties, family, job, length of residence. Seriousness of the crime is not a consideration.

a. all three statements are false
b. only statements 1 & 2 are false
c. only statements 2 & 3 are false
d. only statements 1 & 3 are false
e. all three statements are true

83. What are the three most prevalent types of bonds?

a. cash bonds, surety bonds, and supersedeas bonds
b. cash bonds, surety bonds, and automobile bonds
c. cash bonds, surety bonds, and bank bonds
d. cash bonds, bank bonds, and automobile bonds
e. surety bonds, supersedeas bonds, and bank bonds

84. It is proper for a correctional officer to recommend a bail/bonds person only if requested to do so by an accused.

a. true
b. false

85. An appropriate correctional officer should evaluate an accused person's eligibility for bond by doing which of the following?

a. identify the charge(s) and ask the arresting officer if he or she believes bond is appropriate
b. review the schedule of charges to determine the corresponding bond amount
c. ask the accused to submit a copy of the previous year's federal income tax records to determine whether the accused has the financial ability to make bond
d. allow the accused to telephone the head judge of the circuit and request him or her to set bond
e. a & b above only

86. Which of the following terms refers to an item (e. g., intoxicating beverages, drugs, firearms, or other/weapons) that poses a serious threat to the security of an institution.

a. contraband
b. hard/hazardous contraband
c. nuisance contraband
d. corporal contraband
e. instrumentality

87. Which of the following terms refers to an item which is normally authorized for possession, but which is prohibited if it is altered.

a. contraband
b. hard/hazardous contraband
c. nuisance contraband

d. corporal contraband
e. instrumentality

88. Why is it important to control contraband in a correctional institution or facility?

a. for security purposes
b. for safety of life
c. for safety of property
d. for proper sanitation
e. all of the above

89. Which is NOT a common method of smuggling contraband into a correctional facility?

a. exchanged through a kiss from a visitor
b. sent through the mail in a letter or a package
c. contraband sent underneath a stamp on a letter
d. air drops into open recreation areas from low flying planes
e. none of the above

90. It is not uncommon for employees to smuggle contraband into a correctional facility by hiding items in lunch pails, brief cases, or on their person.

a. true
b. false

91. Common ways to detect contraband include all of the following EXCEPT which one?

a. searches of mail and packages
b. searches of visitors
c. frisk and strip searches of inmates
d. cell and area searches
e. strip searches of staff

92. What is heroin classified as?

a. narcotic
b. depressant
c. stimulant
d. hallucinogen
e. prescription drug

93. Into what category of drugs does alcohol fall?

a. narcotic
b. depressant
c. stimulant
d. hallucinogen
e. inhalant

94. How are amphetamines, methamphetamines, and cocaine categorized?

a. narcotics
b. depressants
c. stimulants
d. hallucinogens
e. inhalants

95. What are aerosol propellants categorized as when they are used improperly?

a. narcotics
b. depressants
c. stimulants
d. hallucinogens
e. inhalants

96. LSD, DMT, STP, and mescaline are categorized as what?

a. narcotics
b. depressants
c. stimulants
d. hallucinogens
e. inhalants

97. When an inmate uses the term "Mary Jane" or "reefer," he or she is probably talking about which of the following?

a. cannabis
b. valium
c. heroin
d. cocaine
e. roofies

98. When an inmate refers to "snow" or "speed," what is he or she talking about?

a. cannabis
b. valium
c. heroin
d. cocaine/methamphetamine
e. none of the above

99. The term "acid" refers to which of the following?

a. narcotic
b. depressant
c. stimulant
d. hallucinogen
e. inhalant

100. Evaluate the following statements:

1. A correctional officer should taste or smell any material suspected of being contraband in order to determine what the substance actually is.

2. A correctional officer should not handle a suspected substance more than what is absolutely necessary and should wash his or her hands thoroughly as soon as possible after handling.

3. A correctional officer should handle and store all chemical materials with care. He or she should tag and identify the substance as to date, time, area, and inmate from whom it was collected.

a. all three statements are true
b. only statements 1 & 2 are true
c. only statements 2 & 3 are true
d. only statements 1 & 3 are true
e. all three statements are false

101. The training required to ensure obedience to established rules is known as what?

a. punishment
b. proactive discipline
c. reactive discipline
d. sanctions
e. retribution

102. Action taken in response to a violation of established rules is known as what?

a. punishment
b. proactive discipline
c. reactive discipline
d. sanctions
e. retribution

103. Which of the following refers to the penalty associated with a rule violation?

a. punishment
b. proactive discipline
c. reactive discipline
d. sanctions
e. retribution

104. The three purposes of discipline are control, punishment, and reaction.

a. true
b. false

105. Evaluate the following statements:

1. The goal of discipline is to maintain order within the correctional facility.

2. The goal of discipline is to protect the safety and welfare of those who live and work in the correctional facility.

3. The goal of discipline is to punish inmates and psychologically condition them to the fact that they are inmates.

a. all three statements are true
b. only statements 1 & 2 are true
c. only statements 2 & 3 are true
d. only statements 1 & 3 are true
e. all three statements are false

106. Which Amendment to the U. S. Constitution prohibits cruel and unusual punishment?

a. First
b. Fourth
c. Fifth
d. Sixth
e. Eighth

107. Which Florida Statute permits humane and reasonable punishments as necessary?

a. 951. 07
b. 951. 17
c. 950. 09
d. 316. 072
e. 316. 189

Disregard this question as the Florida Legislature has rescinded this portion of the statute.

108. Which Florida Statute prohibits corporal punishment?

a. 951. 07
b. 951. 17
c. 950. 09
d. 316. 072
e. 316. 189

Disregard this question as the Florida Legislature has rescinded this portion of the statute.

109. Which Florida Statute makes willful inhumanity and oppression upon any prisoner a second-degree misdemeanor?

a. 951. 07
b. 951. 17
c. 950. 09
d. 316. 072
e. 316. 189

110. Methods of preventive discipline would include which of the following?

a. effective initial orientation
b. withholding food, housing, and medical attention
c. sufficient exercise and recreation
d. corporal punishment
e. a & c above only

111. Refusing to clean a cell, wasting food, refusing to work, or being insolent or disrespectful are examples of minor offenses. Which of the following actions would normally be the most appropriate response?

a. give the inmate a verbal or written reprimand
b. place the inmate in solitary confinement
c. transfer the inmate to a maximum confinement facility
d. confine the inmate to his or her cell
e. all of the above

112. Interfering with a count, attempting to escape, possessing a weapon, or attacking an officer or another inmate are examples of major offenses. Which of the following actions would normally be the most appropriate response?

a. give the inmate a verbal or written reprimand
b. disciplinary confinement
c. loss of "gain time"
d. award of "gain time"
e. b & c above only

113. The correctional officer's role in the disciplinary process includes all of the following EXCEPT which one?

a. serve on the disciplinary hearing committee as required
b. use physical force whenever possible to subdue a violent inmate
c. advise inmates that disciplinary action will result from rule violations
d. write incident reports when warranted
e. know rules and regulations thoroughly

114. Discipline is to be administered:

a. consistently
b. professionally
c. at a prolonged time after the incident
d. a & b above only
e. b & c above only

115. Evaluate the following statements:

1. Hearing officers have the authority to punish inmates.

2. Correctional officers have the authority to punish inmates.

3. Other inmates have the authority to punish inmates.

a. all three statements are true
b. only statement 1 is true
c. only statement 2 is true
d. only statements 1 & 2 are true
e. all three statements are false

116. Evaluate the following statements:

1. The disciplinary hearing committee has the responsibility to gather facts.

2. The disciplinary hearing committee has the responsibility to evaluate the situation.

3. The disciplinary committee has the responsibility to reach a final disposition.

a. all three statements are true
b. only statement 1 is true
c. only statement 2 is true
d. only statements 1 & 3 are true
e. all three statements are false

117. Evaluate the following statements:

1. When the disciplinary hearing committee makes a recommendation, the next level of authority can accept that finding without further review.

2. When the disciplinary hearing committee makes a recommendation, the next level of authority can modify that finding upward.

3. When the disciplinary hearing committee makes a recommendation, the next level of authority can reject that finding.

a. all three statements are true
b. only statement 1 is true
c. only statement 2 is true
d. only statements 1 & 3 are true
e. all three statements are false

118. Removing an inmate from the general inmate population, not for punishment purposes, but simply to ensure his or her safety would be an example of which of the following?

a. disciplinary confinement
b. administrative confinement
c. close management
d. housing confinement
e. rehabilitation confinement

119. Removing an inmate from the general inmate population after a disciplinary hearing committee finds him or her guilty of violating a rule or regulation would be an example of which of the following?

a. disciplinary confinement
b. administrative confinement
c. close management
d. housing confinement
e. rehabilitation confinement

120. Confining an inmate to his or her cell for a lengthy period of time because the inmate's behavior demonstrates an inability to live in the general population would be an example of which of the following?

a. disciplinary confinement
b. administrative confinement
c. close management
d. housing confinement
e. rehabilitation confinement

121. An inmate might be placed in administrative confinement

a. upon disposition of the disciplinary hearing committee
b. pending a disciplinary hearing
c. pending classification
d. all of the above
e. b & c above only

122. Which of the following may be denied to an inmate in confinement?

a. telephone for calls to family
b. hygiene
c. visitation privileges
d. access to library materials
e. a & c above only

123. Evaluate the following statements:

1. An inmate must be monitored by a correctional officer at least once every hour.

2. An inmate must be monitored by medical staff once per day.

3. An inmate must be monitored by a chaplain once per week.

a. all three statements are true
b. only statement 1 is true
c. only statement 2 is true
d. only statements 1 & 3 are true
e. all three statements are false

124. Evaluate the following statements:

1. An inmate must be monitored by the superintendent in a state facility once every two weeks.

2. An inmate must be allowed to see a counselor on a daily basis if the inmate makes such a request.

3. An inmate must be monitored by the shift supervisor once per week.

a. all three statements are true
b. only statement 1 is true
c. only statement 2 is true
d. only statements 1 & 3 are true
e. all three statements are false

125. Evaluate the following statements:

1. The officers assigned to work in the confinement unit should be more experienced officers.

2. A backup officer should be present when placing an inmate into a cell or when removing an inmate from a cell.

3. Officers should communicate verbally with each inmate while patrolling.

a. all three statements are true
b. only statements 1 & 2 are true
c. only statements 2 & 3 are true
d. only statements 1 & 3 are true
e. all three statements are false

126. Evaluate the following statements:

1. Officers should search inmates and cells frequently.

2. Officers should allow a trusted inmate to conduct cell searches if the officers are too busy to do it themselves.

3. A lone officer can open or enter a cell occupied by an inmate only if that inmate is classified as nonviolent.

a. all three statements are false
b. only statements 1 & 2 are false
c. only statements 2 & 3 are false
d. only statements 1 & 3 are false
e. all three statements are true

127. Evaluate the following statements:

1. Officers usually have the necessary resources and sufficient time to help inmates with serious problems or needs.

2. Referrals can provide expert assistance to help inmates solve their problems or address their needs.

3. Officers assigned to the control room do not have the resources nor time to help inmates with serious problems or needs.

a. all three statements are true
b. only statements 1 & 2 are true
c. only statements 2 & 3 are true
d. only statements 1 & 3 are true
e. all three statements are false

128. An officer may make a referral for:

a. financial problems
b. emotional problems
c. mental retardation
d. learning difficulties
e. all of the above

129. The step in the referral process in which alternative solutions are identified is called what?

a. assessment of need
b. decision point
c. referral
d. conclusion
e. apex

130. Evaluate the following statements:

1. When interviewing an inmate about his or her needs, one should not make any promises that cannot be kept.

2. When interviewing an inmate about his or her needs, one should not ask the inmate for any suggestions for solving problems.

3. When interviewing an inmate about his or her needs, one should be considerate, positive and professional.

a. all three statements are true
b. only statements 1 & 2 are true
c. only statements 2 & 3 are true
d. only statements 1 & 3 are true
e. all three statements are false

131. Which of the following is NOT a purpose behind conducting regular searches?

a. detect the manufacturing of weapons or any escape devices
b. detect possible attempts to escape
c. discourage theft of and trafficking in institutional stores
d. check for any malicious waste or destruction of institutional property
e. uncover literature from an unauthorized religion

132. Which of the following items of contraband would a corrections officer be looking for when conducting a search of an inmate's cell?

a. weapons
b. money
c. food
d. drugs
e. all of the above

133. Correctional officers use a variety of equipment or tools when conducting a cell or area search. Which of the following items would NOT be useful?

a. flashlight
b. calculator
c. screwdriver
d. mirror or a probing device
e. gloves

134. Evaluate the following statements:

1. When conducting a cell or area search, the officer should remove all keys from the belt and secure them in his or her hand.

2. When conducting a cell or area search, the officer should have the inmate move to one corner of the cell and remain in a seated position.

3. As soon as the officer conducting the cell or area search discovers contraband, he or she should immediately end the search and allow the inmate to continue his or her activities.

a. all three statements are true
b. only statements 1 & 2 are true

c. only statements 2 & 3 are true
d. only statements 1 & 3 are true
e. all three statements are false

135. An inmate's letters and papers are items that should be examined in a cell search, even though they are personal.

a. true
b. false

136. What is the fundamental duty of a correctional officer?

a. keep inmates from escaping
b. keep inmates working
c. safeguard life and property
d. rehabilitate inmates
e. counsel inmates with regard to past mistakes

137. All the following aspects of correctional operations can impact officer survival EXCEPT for which one?

a. proper classification
b. occasional patrol
c. adequate key and tool control
d. proper transporting of inmates
e. frequent counts

138. The purpose of patrol includes all of the following EXCEPT which one?

a. maintain order
b. prevent criminal activity
c. enforce institutional regulations
d. maintain up-to-date legal materials for inmates
e. protect life and property

139. Evaluate the following statements regarding the specific objectives of preventive patrol.

1. One purpose of preventive patrol is to detect escape attempts, disturbances, or potential trouble.

2. A purpose of preventive patrol is to detect fires, locate any tampering with institution equipment, and become aware of any suicide attempts.

3. One purpose behind preventive patrol is to detect any illegal activities, locate inmates with emotional or medical problems, and to deter sexual assaults.

a. all three statements are true
b. only statement 1 & 2 are true
c. only statement 2 & 3 are true
d. only statement 1 & 3 are true
e. all three statements are false

140. Evaluate the following statements:

1. Do not patrol with a regular or routine pattern or time schedule.

2. Stop and listen before turning corners or approaching "blind spots" when on patrol.

3. Warn officers on other shifts about inmate plans to cause trouble.

a. all three statements are true
b. only statements 1 & 2 are true
c. only statements 2 & 3 are true
d. only statements 1 & 3 are true
e. all three statements are false

141. Evaluate the following statements:

1. Officers should rely solely on audio-visual monitoring devices to maintain surveillance.

2. Corrections officers should be alert at all times for suspicious activity or things out of place.

3. Correction officers should listen to inmates and warn officers on other shifts about rumors of plans to cause trouble.

a. all three statements are true
b. only statements 1 & 2 are true
c. only statements 2 & 3 are true
d. only statements 1 & 3 are true
e. all three statements are false

142. Which of the following is NOT a sign of potential problems that an officer may come across while on patrol?

a. clothesline with clothing hanging on it strung from one side of a cell to the other
b. inmates who avert their eyes when an officer looks at them
c. draped blanket hanging from the top bunk so that it covers the bottom bunk
d. conversation continues when an officer approaches inmates
e. inmates who are extremely quiet, appear to be depressed or angry, or exhibit mood changes

143. Racial or ethnic slurs being shouted by inmates at each other or at officers is not normally considered a sign of potential problems because this is normal "horse-play" in a correctional setting.

a. true
b. false

144. Evaluate the following statements:

1. Prior to going on duty, an officer should make sure he or she is properly uniformed and equipped.

2. Prior to going on duty, an officer should be briefed about activities that have taken place since his or her previous tour of duty.

3. Prior to going on duty, an officer should familiarize himself or herself with activity reports from the local police and/or sheriff's departments.

a. all three statements are true
b. only statements 1 & 2 are true
c. only statements 2 & 3 are true
d. only statements 1 & 3 are true
e. all three statements are false

145. Which of the following is NOT a hazard inherent to a patrol setting?

a. physical attack
b. getting hit by thrown objects
c. being taken hostage
d. injury resulting from responding to emergency situations
e. all are hazards

146. Common hazards inherent in vehicle patrol in a correctional setting include vehicle accidents and assaults by other correctional officers.

a. true
b. false

147. The process of organizing and attaching meaning to sensations so that the sensations can be interpreted as part of observation is known as what?

a. perception
b. practice
c. prejudice
d. preconception
e. observation

148. The accurate noting of what is presented to the five senses through keeping in view, taking notice of, or giving attention to persons, things, or circumstances is known as what?

a. perception
b. practice
c. prejudice
d. preconception
e. observation

149. What are the three parts of a complete observation?

a. receiving a stimulus, evaluating the stimulus, and responding to the stimulus
b. receiving a stimulus, being aware of the stimulus, and evaluating the stimulus
c. receiving a stimulus, being aware of the stimulus, and responding to the stimulus
d. sending a stimulus, being aware of the stimulus, and responding to the stimulus
e. none of the above

150. Evaluate the following statements:

1. It is more difficult to see slow-moving objects at night.

2. Stationary objects are not noticed as well from the corner of the eye.

3. Movement is not noticed nearly as well from the corner of the eye as from straight on.

a. all three statements are true
b. only statement 1 is true
c. only statements 1 & 2 are true
d. only statement 3 is true
e. all three statements are false

151. Upon which of the following does visual acuity largely depend?

a. proximity
b. size
c. light conditions
d. all of the above
e. b & c above only

152. How close does an observer have to be to a person for visual recognition of features under the condition of full moonlight?

a. 2 to 3 yards
b. 3 to 5 yards

c. 6 to 8 yards
d. 10 to 11 yards
e. 12 to 14 yards

153. Blue objects will appear ______ when red and blue objects are compared.

a. smaller
b. larger
c. more distinct
d. more distant
e. blurred

154. Depth perception requires:

a. good lighting conditions
b. close proximity
c. proper coordination of both eyes
d. the object sighted upon must be of a light color
e. a horizontal position of the objected sighted in relation to the viewer

155. Visual observation and perception are affected by "mental set."

a. true
b. false

156. Evaluate the following statements:

1. Sounds carry a greater distance at night.

2. Sounds carry a shorter distance at night.

3. An object that makes noises will appear smaller.

a. all three statements are true
b. only statement 1 is true
c. only statements 1 & 2 are true
d. only statement 3 is true
e. all three statements are false

157. Evaluate the following statements:

1. Many substances can be identified by their odors

2. Certain substances such, as gasoline and ether, will temporarily deaden sense of smell

3. Nasal congestion will reduce sense of smell

a. all three statements are true
b. only statement 1 is true
c. only statements 1 & 2 are true
d. only statement 3 is true
e. all three statements are false

158. Evaluate the following statements:

1. The sense of touch can be used to identify many objects or situations of importance

2. The sense of touch can be affected by abnormal positions

3. The sense of touch is seldom, if ever, affected by adaption

a. all three statements are true
b. only statement 1 is true
c. only statements 1 & 2 are true
d. only statement 3 is true
e. all three statements are false

159. Evaluate the following statements:

1. When making an observation, one should trust what is seen over what is heard if there is an apparent conflict.

2. When making an observation, one should trust what is heard over what is seen when there is an apparent conflict.

3. When making an observation, one should review meanings and interpretations of observations.

a. all three statements are true
b. only statements 1 is true
c. only statements 2 & 3 are true
d. only statements 1 & 3 are true
e. all three statements are false

160. Evaluate the following statements:

1. When dealing with a witness, the officer should realize that attention will focus on the louder or larger element in a given situation.

2. When dealing with a witness, the officer should realize that attention will focus on an object, individual, or element that appears more than once.

3. When dealing with a witness, the officer should realize that attention will focus on movement as opposed to stationary objects or elements.

a. all three statements are true
b. only statements 1 is true
c. only statements 2 & 3 are true
d. only statements 1 & 3 are true
e. all three statements are false

161. What should one do to improve perception and observation?

a. learn what signs or clues to look for in a given situation as a matter of officer interest
b. establish a "big picture" of a person, event, or scene before making more specific analytical observations of details
c. zero in on specific analytical details before establishing a "big picture" of an observation in order to properly evaluate the big picture
d. a & b above only
e. a & c above only

162. Which of the following tools might be considered hazardous (restricted) in a correctional facility?

a. pliers
b. hacksaw blades
c. barber tools
d. a & b above only
e. b & c above only

163. A shadow board is an effective method for displaying and organizing tools. What is a shadow board?

a. the exact size and shape of a tool is drawn on the board where the tool is stored
b. the inventory number of a tool is placed on the board and the tool with the corresponding inventory number is to be placed and stored at that location
c. a colored square is painted at a given location on the board and the tool with the corresponding color code is to be placed and stored at that location
d. none of the above

164. Which of the following is NOT a flammable, hazardous, or poisonous material that must be controlled within a correctional facility?

a. wood alcohol or methyl alcohol
b. pencil lead
c. photocopy fluids
d. glue
e. acids

165. To whom should hazardous materials be issued?

a. only to correctional captains and above
b. only to inmates on a trustee status and staff members
c. only to staff members
d. only to civilian work contract personnel
e. b & d above only

166. Evaluate the following statements with regard to why a key control system is necessary.

1. A key control system is necessary in order to prevent escapes or a takeover of the facility.

2. A key control system is necessary to control property such as tools and weapons.

3. A key control system is necessary so as to provide access to keys in an emergency.

a. all three statements are true
b. only statements 1 is true
c. only statements 2 & 3 are true
d. only statements 1 & 3 are true
e. all three statements are false

167. Evaluate the following statements:

1. Keys should be maintained on key rings that close by a clip or spring arrangement and should have metal tags with a hook number.

2. An employee who inadvertently carries a key home should notify the control room promptly.

3. Emergency keys should stored apart from operational keys

a. all three statements are true
b. only statements 1 is true
c. only statements 2 & 3 are true
d. only statements 1 & 3 are true
e. all three statements are false

168. Evaluate the following statements:

1. Employees should be required to sign a receipt when they are issued a key permanently.

2. "Pattern keys" should be issued only to officers who normally work the area where such a key fits.

3. Keys should be issued from multiple sites to make it more convenient for employees.

a. all three statements are true
b. only statements 1 is true
c. only statements 2 & 3 are true
d. only statements 1 & 3 are true
e. all three statements are false

169. Evaluate the following statements:

1. Officers should carry and use keys inconspicuously.

2. Officers should refer to key numbers for security reasons when they are in the presence of inmates.

3. Officers should never carry keys to both inside and outside doors at the same time.

a. all three statements are true
b. only statements 1 is true
c. only statements 2 & 3 are true
d. only statements 1 & 3 are true
e. all three statements are false

170. Inmate counts that are conducted at specific times of the day and night in an organized manner are known as what?

a. formal counts
b. informal, irregular, census checks
c. outcounts
d. transportation counts
e. roll call

171. Which of the following refers to counts that are made while inmates are working or engaged in regular activities?

a. formal counts
b. informal, irregular, census checks
c. outcounts
d. transportation counts
e. roll call

172. Inmate counts that are made at irregular times and reported only when an inmate is missing are known as what?

a. formal counts
b. informal, irregular, census checks
c. outcounts
d. transportation counts
e. roll call

173. Which of the following refers to counts that are not conducted when inmates are in their quarters or accustomed counting areas?

a. formal counts
b. informal, irregular, census checks
c. outcounts
d. transportation counts
e. roll call

174. Which of the following is NOT a principle of counting inmates properly?

a. perform official, formal counts at a minimum of once per day
b. schedule counts so they provide as little interference as possible with daily work and activities
c. do not allow anything, short of an emergency, to interrupt or distract while counting
d. remain in count area until count is verified as correct
e. none of the above

175. Evaluate the following statements:

1. Count slips should be complete and have no erasures.

2. Count slips should have no strikeouts.

3. Count slips should be written in #2 pencil.

a. all three statements are true
b. only statement 1 is true
c. only statements 1 & 2 are true
d. only statements 2 & 3 are true
e. all three statements are false

176. What is a "sally port?"

a. a glass enclosed area that is open on one side
b. an area enclosed by iron bars but which is open on one side
c. the foyer area of a facility administration building
d. a double gate
e. the opening in a cell door that accommodates the delivery of a food tray

177. Evaluate the following statements:

1. The officer should close the outer gate of a sally port after traffic (persons or vehicles) has cleared the gate threshold.

2. The officer should open the inner gate of a sally port only after the outer gate has closed. Both gates should never be open at the same time.

3. The officer should close the inner gate of a sally port after traffic (persons or vehicles) has cleared the gate threshold.

a. all three statements are true
b. only statement 1 is true

c. only statements 1 & 2 are true
d. only statements 2 & 3 are true
e. all three statements are false

178. Which of the following refers to a manually operated security lock which cannot be slam locked and requires a key to open and lock?

a. automatic spring and deadlock system
b. simple deadlock system
c. combination spring and deadlock system
d. complex deadlock system
e. none of the above

179. Which of the following refers to a manually operated security lock that allows you to slam lock without a key but does require a key to open and place on deadlock?

a. automatic spring and deadlock system
b. simple deadlock system
c. combination spring and deadlock system
d. complex deadlock system
e. none of the above

180. Factors that control inmate movement include which of the following?

a. physical design of facility
b. security control points
c. weather
d. temperature
e. a & b above only

181. How should a correctional officer position himself or herself when escorting an inmate within the facility?

a. walk behind the inmate, offset slightly to the right or left, and stay out of the inmate's reach
b. lead the inmate by walking in front, but advise the inmate to stay three steps behind the officer
c. keep the inmate apart from other persons
d. handcuff the right wrist of the inmate to the left wrist of the officer
e. a & c above only

182. Evaluate the following statements:

1. A preliminary investigation is directed at establishing whether a criminal act has been committed and, if so, what type of a criminal act.

2. An investigation is best described as making detailed and systematic inquiries and/or observations.

3. Some sources of information that can be utilized during a criminal investigation are the crime scene, scientific aids, people, state agencies, and local agencies.

a. all three statements are true
b. only statements 1 & 2 are true
c. only statements 1 & 3 are true
d. only statements 2 & 3 are true
e. all three statements are false

183. What is the purpose of conducting a preliminary investigation?

a. gather information after the initial report to build a case
b. make detailed and systematic inquiries and/or observations
c. identify the impact of a crime
d. establish whether a criminal act has been committed and, if so, what type
e. provide information for a "Victim Impact Statement" in court

184. Which of the following is NOT a key element of a preliminary investigation?

a. determine if a crime has been committed
b. determine the modus operandi of a suspect
c. preserve the integrity of the crime scene
d. document case information
e. gather evidence

185. A preliminary survey is conducted for which of the following reasons?

a. determine overall picture
b. organize search procedures
c. establish objectives and give specific assignments
d. determine the best method of search
e. all of the above

186. Which of the following terms refers to the gathering of information subsequent to the initial report to help further establish a case?

a. later investigation
b. post-investigation
c. extended investigation
d. preliminary investigation
e. follow-up investigation

187. Which of the following procedures would not normally be considered during a follow-up investigation?

a. modus operandi
b. review offense reports
c. determine whether a crime has taken place
d. tape statements
e. show-up

188. Provided there are no injured persons at the crime scene, what is the first officer's primary responsibility?

a. gather up all obvious evidence
b. protect the crime scene
c. interview witnesses
d. console or calm the victim
e. start looking for the perpetrator

189. Which following item is NOT a step in a properly conducted crime scene search?

a. protecting the crime scene
b. photographing the overall crime scene and the physical evidence located therein
c. conducting a detailed search of the crime scene for evidence
d. setting forth a physical description of the suspect
e. documenting all physical evidence

190. When the crime scene investigator arrives at the scene, what is the first thing he or she should do?

a. debrief officers already on the scene
b. conduct a preliminary survey
c. secure the area
d. make a press release
e. immediately advise the superior of what he or she has

191. One primary responsibility of the first officer to arrive is to determine the extent of the crime scene. What should the initial officer do to accomplish this goal?

a. ask for volunteers to help locate any pertinent evidence
b. limit the size of the crime scene and expand it later only if necessary
c. do not limit the size of the crime scene
d. honor any media requests to enter the area under the First Amendment
e. invite media representatives into the crime scene in the hopes that more eyes will uncover more evidence

192. The responsibilities of the first officer arriving at the scene of a crime include which of the following items?

1. administering first aid
2. arresting the suspect
3. protecting evidence
4. calling the State Attorney's Office

a. 1, 2, 3 but not 4
b. 2, 3, 4 but not 1
c. 1, 3, 4 but not 2
d. 1, 2, 4 but not 3
e. neither 1, 2, 3, or 4

193. What are the five fundamental methods of searching a crime scene?

a. strip or line pattern, grid, spiral, quadrant or zone, and block method
b. strip or line pattern, block, grid, spiral, quadrant or zone, and pie or wheel patterns
c. strip or line pattern, grid, spot, quadrant or zone, and pie or wheel patterns
d. strip or line pattern, grid, spiral, quadrant or zone, and pie or wheel patterns
e. aerial, spot, quadrant or zone, ground-level, and pie patterns

194. Which of the following areas have had the most impact on evidence?

1. legal requirements
2. scientific value
3. court presentation
4. jurisprudence in other countries

a. 1 and 2
b. 1 and 3
c. 2 and 3
d. 1 and 4
e. 3 and 4

195. The responsibilities of the officer who is gathering evidence include which of the following items?

1. marking evidence
2. tagging evidence
3. evaluating evidence

4. controlling the crime lab
5. clearing the scene

a. all but 1
b. all but 2
c. all but 3
d. all but 4
e. all but 5

196. Which of the following is NOT one of the three major evidence collection faults?

a. failure to submit sufficient quantities of evidence
b. failure to submit the suspect's clothing
c. failure to submit known standards of evidence
d. failure to protect the evidence from contamination
e. failure to maintain chain of custody

197. The witnessed, written record of all individuals who have maintained unbroken control over an item of evidence since its acquisition is known as what?

a. voir dire
b. nolle prosequi
c. chain of custody
d. chain of evidence
e. contendere nolo

198. Components of the "chain of custody" would include which of the following?

1. whoever had contact with the evidence
2. time evidence was handled
3. circumstances under which evidence was handled
4. what changes, if any, were made to the evidence

a. 1, 2, and 3
b. 1, 3, and 4
c. 2, 3, and 4
d. 1, 2, 3, and 4
e. 3 and 4

199. Evaluate the following statements with regard to rules and regulations relevant to corrections.

1. The provisions contained in Florida Statutes that deal with corrections are further expanded by rules of the 2nd District Court of Appeal.

2. The provisions contained in Florida Statutes that deal with corrections are further expanded by rules in the Florida Administrative Code.

3. Florida Statutes authorize the Department of Corrections to promulgate rules governing the administration of the correctional system and the operation of the Department.

a. all three statements are true
b. only statements 1 & 2 are true
c. only statements 1 & 3 are true
d. only statements 2 & 3 are true
e. all three statements are false

200. Where are the rules that govern the administration of Florida's correctional system and the Department of Corrections located?

a. Chapter 33, Florida Administrative Code
b. Chapter 37, Florida Administrative Code
c. Chapter 23, Florida Statutes
d. Chapter 13, Florida Administrative Code
e. Chapter 33, Florida Statutes

Chapter 4 Answer Key

1. C
2. D
3. B
4. B
5. D
6. E
7. C
8. E
9. D
10. E
11. D
12. A
13. C
14. E
15. C
16. B
17. B
18. A
19. D
20. B
21. D
22. E
23. D
24. E
25. A
26. D
27. C
28. A
29. B
30. A
31. D
32. D
33. E
34. C
35. E
36. D
37. B
38. A
39. B
40. A
41. E
42. B
43. D
44. B
45. D
46. B
47. B
48. A
49. D
50. A
51. A
52. A
53. A
54. C
55. D
56. A
57. B
58. D
59. E
60. D
61. E
62. C
63. B
64. D
65. E
66. D
67. A
68. A
69. B
70. A
71. C
72. E
73. E
74. C
75. A
76. E
77. A
78. D
79. D
80. A
81. D
82. C
83. A
84. B
85. E
86. B
87. C
88. E
89. D
90. A
91. E
92. A
93. B
94. C
95. E
96. D
97. A
98. D
99. D
100. C
101. B
102. C
103. A
104. B
105. B
106. E
~~107. A~~
~~108. B~~
109. C
110. E
111. A
112. E
113. B
114. D
115. B
116. A
117. D
118. B
119. A
120. C
121. E
122. E
123. A
124. E
125. A
126. C
127. C
128. E
129. B
130. D
131. E
132. E
133. B
134. A
135. E
136. C
137. B
138. D
139. A
140. A
141. C
142. D
143. B
144. B
145. E
146. B
147. A
148. E
149. C
150. C
151. D
152. D
153. B
154. C
155. A
156. B
157. A
158. C
159. D
160. A
161. D
162. E
163. A
164. B
165. C
166. A
167. C
168. B
169. D
170. A
171. B
172. B
173. C
174. A
175. C
176. D
177. A
178. B
179. C
180. E
181. E
182. A
183. D
184. B
185. E
186. E
187. C
188. B
189. D
190. B
191. C
192. A
193. D
194. A
195. D
196. B
197. C
198. D
199. D
200. A

CHAPTER 5

COMMUNICATIONS AND INTERPERSONAL SKILLS II

Chapter Overview

This portion of the study guide centers around the inmate world. The social world inside a correctional facility is made up of a complex web of customs and behaviors. Some inmate habits may seem barbaric or aberrant to people who are not familiar with the field of corrections. However, these practices are regular fixtures in the inmate world. While the material here is far from being definitive and will not transform you into an instant expert, it does sensitize potential officers to what goes on inside the walls.

Maintaining control and ensuring order are fundamental concerns in any correctional operation. Responsible officers know the true value of report writing and case preparation. As a result, some of our attention will also focus on these aspects of a corrections officer's job.

The questions that follow reflect the goals and objectives that form the corrections academy curriculum. By the time you complete this section, you should have a firm understanding of the following topics:

- Human Adjustment to Imprisonment
- Inmate Societies
- Criminal Types and Careers
- Institutional Criminalities
- Female Inmates
- Inmate Homosexuality
- Supervision Techniques
- Recognizing Inmate Deception and Manipulation
- Note Taking
- Taking Statements
- Report Writing
- Reporting Procedures
- Radio Procedures, Equipmen,t and Codes
- Florida Crime Information Center (FCIC)

Questions

1. Which of the following terms best characterizes prison society?
   a. forced equality
   b. forced segregation
   c. voluntary segregation
   d. forced management
   e. forced supervision

2. Which of the following factors is NOT a deprivation that causes problems for individuals who are imprisoned?
   a. autonomy
   b. relative freedom from rules
   c. homosexual relationships
   d. heterosexual relationships
   e. goods and services

3. Psychological and material deprivations jeopardize all of the following except which one?
   a. self-esteem
   b. personal defense systems and social adaptation
   c. social class
   d. heterosexuality
   e. emotional security

4. Which of the following does NOT affect an individual's ability to adjust to imprisonment?
   a. age
   b. social class
   c. criminal career
   d. religious preference
   e. none of the above

5. Evaluate the following statements:
   1. Some inmates adjust to the deprivation of goods and services in prison by running a "store."
   2. Some inmates adjust to the deprivation of heterosexual relationships in prison by engaging in homosexual activities.
   3. Rationalization is one defense mechanism that inmates may utilize when adjusting to imprisonment.

   a. all three statements are true
   b. only statements 1 & 2 are true
   c. only statements 1 & 3 are true
   d. only statements 2 & 3 are true
   e. all three statements are false

6. Which of the following items does NOT characterize the typical inmate population?
   a. well educated
   b. come from society's lower social and economic levels
   c. may come from broken homes
   d. young, unmarried males
   e. gang members

7. Evaluate the following statements:
   1. The main purpose of an inmate social system is to provide a social network for prisoners.
   2. An important purpose of an inmate social system is to protect inmates against further isolation.
   3. The "inmate code" stresses loyalty to other inmates within the group.

   a. all three statements are true
   b. only statements 1 & 2 are true
   c. only statements 1 & 3 are true
   d. only statements 2 & 3 are true
   e. all three statements are false

8. Which of the following is NOT a concern of a facility with regard to prison gangs ?
   a. transfer of control from prison authorities to a small group of inmates
   b. decreased narcotics and other illegal contraband within a prison
   c. protection rackets
   d. homosexual prostitution
   e. cults or other fanatical groups

9. Which of the following best describes the typical career criminal?
   a. armed robber
   b. one-time loser
   c. naive check forger
   d. property offender
   e. violent offender

10. Which is NOT a characteristic of a "professional thief"?
    a. may be involved in confidence games
    b. may be involved in burglary and shoplifting

c. has frequent contacts with the underworld
d. seldom does time in prison because he or she is clever enough to avoid getting arrested
e. all of the above

11. Evaluate the following statements:

1. A professional "heavy" criminal is highly skilled, is tied to team or mob operations, and satisfied with that lifestyle.

2. A semiprofessional property criminal has limited skills, but tries to pull off spectacular "crime of the century" acts.

3. The "naive check forger" is usually an unsophisticated recidivistic check passer.

a. all three statements are true
b. only statements 1 & 2 are true
c. only statements 1 & 3 are true
d. only statements 2 & 3 are true
e. all three statements are false

12. Which of the following terms refers to persons within business and corporate organizations who violate state and regulatory statutes?

a. recidivist criminals
b. professional fringe violators
c. white collar criminals
d. naive check forgers
e. embezzlers

13. Evaluate the following statements:

1. A person who is a member of a legitimate profession and utilizes his or her professional skills to commit crime is called a security violator.

2. A recidivist is a person who desists from further criminal activity.

3. Murderers are an example of a typical career criminal.

a. all three statements are true
b. only statements 1 & 2 are true
c. only statements 1 & 3 are true
d. only statements 2 & 3 are true
e. all three statements are false

14. Which one of the following crimes typically does NOT occur within a correctional setting?

a. blackmail
b. homicide
c. sex crimes
d. mail fraud
e. bribery

15. Crimes within institutional walls can be either a single or a multiple assailant event. Which of the following crimes can fall under both?

a. informing
b. gang phenomena
c. homosexuality
d. arguments
e. riots

16. Which of the following strategies can reduce the crime rate within a correctional setting?

a. heavier reliance upon snitches
b. developing a fear of institutional sanctions within inmates
c. eventual disciplinary sanctions
d. effective contraband control
e. using a telephone "hot line" or a suggestion box so that inmates can make anonymous reports

17. Which of the following contains the steps an officer needs to use when "sizing up a situation" and the order in which these steps need to be accomplished?

a. observe, position, posture, listen
b. listen, observe, position, posture
c. observe, listen, position, posture
d. position, observe, posture, listen
e. position, listen, observe, posture

18. The major elements of positioning include which of the following?

a. keeping a safe distance
b. being able to see and hear groups and individuals
c. eye contact
d. facing squarely
e. all of the above

19. Which of the following usually is NOT something an officer might look for when first coming on shift ?

a. weather
b. usual inmate routine
c. grouping of inmates
d. changes in inmate physical appearance
e. none of the above

20. Holding your body in such a way to show strength, confidence, interest and control is known as what?
    a. listening
    b. observing
    c. posturing
    d. positioning
    e. demeanor

21. Clues that can be used to develop inferences include all of the following except:
    a. values
    b. relationships
    c. energy levels
    d. decibel ratings
    e. feeling cues

22. Active involvement in most activities would produce which category of energy levels?
    a. zero
    b. low
    c. moderate
    d. high
    e. none of the above

23. Which of the following refers to the three basic environments of every individual ?
    a. where a person lives, works, and learns
    b. where a person sleeps, works, and eats
    c. where a person reflects, regroups, and reinvigorates
    d. where a person recharges, regroups, and realizes
    e. where a person integrates, initiates, and insulates

24. Evaluate the following statements:
    1. Inferences are more likely to be accurate if they are based on detailed and concrete observations rather than on vague, general ones.
    2. The steps involved in listening include suspending judgment, picking out key words, identifying the intensity of what is said, and reflecting on mood.
    3. The skill of seeing and hearing what is really happening and the ability to mirror that understanding back to the individual is an example of responding to content.

    a. all three statements are true
    b. only statements 1 & 2 are true
    c. only statements 2 & 3 are true
    d. only statements 1 & 3 are true
    e. all three statements are false

25. Evaluate the following statements:
    1. Volume, emotion, and pitch are vocal characteristics that may be used to determine intensity.
    2. The ability to capture in words the specific feelings being presented by an inmate is called "responding to feeling."
    3. If a communication interchange goes deeper than what the officer feels he or she can manage, it is appropriate to refer the inmate to a counselor or other specialist.

    a. all three statements are true
    b. only statements 1 & 2 are true
    c. only statements 2 & 3 are true
    d. only statements 1 & 3 are true
    e. all three statements are false

26. Which of the following is a component of the 5WH method?
    a. asking why
    b. asking who
    c. asking how
    d. asking when
    e. all of the above

27. Which of the following refers to the ability to make sense out of an inmate's answers, recognizing the answers not spoken, and thinking carefully about what the inmate has said in answering a question?
    a. reflecting on answers and recycle
    b. controlling behavior
    c. reflection on feeling and meaning
    d. communication interchange
    e. responding to feeling and meaning

28. Questions like "What did he or she say?" or "How does he or she look?" are questions that one uses when doing what?
    a. controlling behavior
    b. handling a request
    c. reinforcing behavior
    d. reflecting
    e. contemplating

29. Taking charge to assure appropriate behavior that serves the interests of the institution, the staff member and the inmate defines which of the following?

 a. reinforcing behavior
 b. responding to feeling and meaning
 c. controlling behavior
 d. observing behavior
 e. manipulative behavior

30. Checking things out and then giving a response accompanied with a reason is an example of which of the following?

 a. handling requests
 b. controlling behavior
 c. reflecting
 d. responding to meaning
 e. observing behavior

31. Evaluate the following statements:

 1. One reason for giving an inmate a reason for your response is so that the inmate will know the reason for granting a request, but will understand that a future request may not be granted if reasons are not as good.

 2. A "mild request format" means that an inmate does not care whether he or she is granted the request.

 3. "Softening a request" or toning it down and making it more palatable is what a supervisor should do after if a corrections officer refuses to comply with a direct order.

 a. all three statements are false
 b. only statements 1 & 2 are false
 c. only statements 1 & 3 are false
 d. only statements 2 & 3 are false
 e. all three statements are true

32. Administering punishments and distributing rewards effectively so as to show inmates the positive and negative consequences of their actions is known as what?

 a. softening a request
 b. controlling behavior
 c. responding to feeling and meaning
 d. deterrence
 e. reinforcing behavior

33. Evaluate the following statements:

 1. The phrase "human actions determine human reactions" means that if inmates are treated like the human beings they are, then more decent and constructive behavior will be promoted.

 2. The elements of reinforcing behavior include both positive and negative reinforcement.

 3. Since nonverbal reinforcers usually involve the use of force, they should be used as a last resort.

 a. all three statements are true
 b. only statements 1 & 2 are true
 c. only statements 1 & 3 are true
 d. only statements 2 & 3 are true
 e. all three statements are false

34. Which of the following is NOT a behavioral characteristic exhibited by female inmates?

 a. low self-esteem
 b. freely expresses anger, fear, affection, especially verbally
 c. separation from family causes formation of surrogate families within the institution
 d. homosexual activities are more for gratification than for companionship and affection
 e. depression, guilt, worry over care and custody of children

35. Which of the following is NOT a special need of female inmates?

 a. need to improve decision-making skills to increase dependency
 b. need same range and quality of training programs as do male inmates
 c. need response and visitation from family and friends
 d. have specialized health needs
 e. improve job-related skills

36. In terms of intake, housing, and supervision of female inmates in Florida, which is NOT a legal consideration?

 a. female inmates must be housed separately from male inmates
 b. a female officer must be present to admit and process female inmate
 c. a female employee must be on duty at all times when the facility houses female inmates
 d. male employees must be accompanied by a female employee when entering a female

housing area unless an emergency situation dictates otherwise

e. none of the above

37. Which of the following terms refers to voluntary homosexuality that developed before entering the correctional institution?

a. situational homosexuality
b. lifestyle homosexuality
c. coerced homosexuality
d. deviant career
e. emasculation

38. Evaluate the following statements:

1. "Situational homosexuality" refers to homosexuality that develops inside the institution through coercion, force, or by choice through the lack of appropriate sexual release.

2. Health hazards typically associated with homosexual behavior, such as venereal disease and AIDS, are not present since the institution is a closed population.

3. Suicide is a distinct effect of lifestyle homosexuality.

a. all three statements are false
b. only statements 1 & 2 are false
c. only statements 1 & 3 are false
d. only statements 2 & 3 are false
e. all three statements are true

39. Which of the following is NOT an institutional factor that contributes to homosexual behavior?

a. housing younger inmates with older inmates
b. a single sex environment
c. meaningful work and recreational activities
d. demands of the prison "caste system"
e. presence of homosexual prostitutes

40. All the following items are guidelines aimed at controlling homosexual behavior in a correctional facility, except one. Which one is not such a guideline?

a. supervise shower activities closely
b. encourage feminine/masculine traits among male/female inmates
c. encourage inmate to participate in recreational activities as outlets for their energies
d. keep all cell windows and bars clear
e. check to make sure inmates are in their assigned areas

41. Evaluate the following statements:

1. Failure to recognize individual differences among inmates is the most common supervising error in the correctional field.

2. One consequence of poor supervision is superior inmate morale.

3. Supervision is the action, process or occupation of overseeing and directing in order to accomplish tasks(s).

a. all three statements are true
b. only statements 1 & 2 are true
c. only statements 1 & 3 are true
d. only statements 2 & 3 are true
e. all three statements are false

42. Which of the following is NOT an area of special concern when supervising inmates ?

a. administrative offices
b. dining room
c. chapel
d. clinic or sick bay
e. recreational area

43. Evaluate the following statements:

1. The phrase "firm, but fair" would be an example of a practice that enhances the chances of positive effects when supervising inmates.

2. "Avoid familiarity with inmates" is an example of a bad supervisory practice.

3. Showing favoritism to one inmate makes supervision easier since it lets other inmates know they have somebody else to turn to if the need arises.

a. all three statements are false
b. only statements 1 & 2 are false
c. only statements 1 & 3 are false
d. only statements 2 & 3 are false
e. all three statements are true

44. Which of the following is NOT a good general rule for a supervisor to follow when dealing with inmates ?

a. give limited advice to inmates
b. never make a promise you cannot keep
c. do not gossip with inmates
d. avoid familiarity with inmates
e. do not discuss other staff members with inmates

45. Which of the following is a good supervisory technique to use in an institutional facility ?

a. an inmate is more likely to do something if he or she understands the reason for the action
b. coercion to instill fear of noncompliance
c. bullying or belittlement because they show inmates who is in charge
d. using profanity or vulgarity to give emphasis to what one is saying
e. letting inmates vote on an item makes them more responsible

46. Correctional officers need to be aware of several common tactics that inmates employ. Which of the following is NOT one of those inmate tactics?

a. discussing an officer's personal life
b. playing one officer against another
c. expecting favors in return for information
d. trying to blackmail officers who grant favors
e. all of the above are common inmate tactics

47. Why do inmates engage in manipulation and deception of staff ?

a. to gain status among peers
b. to gain control and autonomy
c. for personal reward and gain
d. to gain control over staff members
e. all of the above are reasons

48. Which of the following practices should alert a corrections officer to the possibility that an inmate is trying to manipulate or deceive him or her?

a. overfriendliness of inmate towards the officer
b. sharing rumors concerning the staff member or others
c. requesting personal information
d. excessive praise and flattery
e. all of the above are danger signs

49. Evaluate the following statements:

1. A new or naive correctional officer is an ideal target for inmate deception and manipulation.

2. An inmate who continuously breaks small rules may be testing a correctional officer.

3. An inmate who asks questions or who tries to listen to conversations among staff members may be gathering information about staff for purposes of deception and manipulation.

a. all three statements are true
b. only statements 1 & 2 are true
c. only statements 1 & 3 are true
d. only statements 2 & 3 are true
e. all three statements are false

50. Which of the following is NOT a method that inmates use to gather information about staff for deception and manipulation?

a. asking questions
b. assisting officers with sting operation
c. listening to conversation among staff members
d. watching staff members interact with other inmates
e. watching staff members interact with other staff inmates

51. In discussing the activities of a deception team, which one of the following members spends time befriending the correctional officer and then uses that friendship to coerce the officer into engaging in rule infractions?

a. observer
b. contact
c. runner
d. turner
e. point man

52. In discussing the activities of a deception team, which one of the following members supplies information about the correctional officer's work habits, likes, and dislikes?

a. observer
b. contact
c. runner
d. turner
e. point man

53. In discussing the activities of a deception team, which one of the following members stands guard when the correctional officer is in the process of granting illegal favors, violating institutional rules, or is being compromised or harmed?

a. observer
b. contact
c. runner
d. turner
e. point man

54. Brief notations concerning specific events (i.e., accident, crime, incident, etc.) or a general collection of observations concerning many aspects of a corrections officer's job refers to which of the following terms?

a. interrogation
b. report writing
c. note taking
d. interpersonal communications
e. interviewing

55. Which of the following are good procedures to follow when taking notes?

a. write all information out on scraps of paper and destroy them after the report is written
b. write down the case number, abbreviate, use pencil
c. identify all notes, transfer the statements to the report
d. identify all notes, use sketches, write legibly, be accurate
e. use a notebook, write down the case number, staple notes to the original report

56. Which of the following procedures would be incorrect in note taking?

a. use scraps of paper
b. use ink
c. use freehand sketches, if appropriate
d. use common abbreviations
e. use a notebook

57. Reporting procedures may be found in all of the following documents except one. Which one is that?

a. on the form or report
b. on your field notes
c. in administrative rules
d. in Florida statutes
e. in agency policy guidelines

58. Which is NOT a use of notes?

a. admission as evidence
b. circumvents the need for writing a report
c. subject to scrutiny of the contents
d. serves as a general index to help an officer's memory
e. used to refresh memory

59. Which of the following kinds of information are NOT entered into a notebook?

a. names of victims, witnesses, suspects
b. circumstances of the incident
c. opinions of the investigating officer
d. report number or file number
e. location of incident

60. In which of the following incidents should a corrections officer obtain statements whenever possible?

a. criminal offenses
b. noncriminal incidents
c. investigative processes
d. inmate escape
e. all of the above

61. When describing suspects, a corrections officer should include all the following factors EXCEPT which one?

a. height and weight
b. race, sex, and age
c. color of hair
d. clothes
e. all of the above should be included

62. When a corrections officer is taking statements at an accident such as an industrial mishap, he or she should include all of the following EXCEPT which one?

a. how to treat the injuries
b. nature and extent of injuries
c. probable cause of injuries
d. seriousness of injuries
e. what was seen or heard

63. In the detailed description of a vehicle, a corrections officer would include all but which one of the following pieces of information?

a. color
b. make and model
c. tag number
d. mileage
e. identifying marks such as dents or bumper stickers

64. Evaluate the following statements:

1. The first procedure to follow when taking statements would be to review the information and its completeness.

2. It is always necessary to administer an oath as a basic procedure in taking statements.

3. A report is a temporary record which communicates important facts to be used in the future.

a. all three statements are false
b. only statements 1 & 2 are false
c. only statements 1 & 3 are false
d. only statements 2 & 3 are false
e. all three statements are true

65. Reports are used for which of the following reasons?

a. investigative leads
b. a permanent record of facts
c. statistical analysis
d. officer evaluations
e. all of the above

66. Which of the following refers to a permanent written record which communicates important facts to be used in the future?

a. note taking
b. interpersonal communications
c. report
d. subpoena
e. affidavit

67. Which of the following steps is NOT included in report writing?

a. gather the facts, write the report, evaluate the report writer's performance
b. gather the facts, record the facts, organize the facts
c. gather the facts, record the facts, conduct follow-up interviews
d. gather the facts, add the officer's opinion, evaluate the report
e. gather the facts, record the facts, testify about case details

68. Which of the following best identifies the basic requirements of a report?

a. complete, concise, confusing, cute
b. complete, concise, legible, opinionated
c. complete, concise, clear, correct
d. complete, irregular, on time, mechanically correct
e. complete, legible, opinionated, humorous where appropriate

69. Which of the following terms refers to the correction of spelling, capitalization, and punctuation errors when checking over a report?

a. dictating
b. editing
c. mechanics of language
d. evaluation
e. proofreading

70. Evaluate the following statements:

1. A sentence is a group of words containing a subject and a verb and expressing a complete thought.

2. Editing is the correction of errors in spelling, capitalization and punctuation.

3. Proofreading is rewriting to improve report content.

a. all three statements are false
b. only statements 1 & 2 are false
c. only statements 1 & 3 are false
d. only statements 2 & 3 are false
e. all three statements are true

71. Which of the following are the "5 W's" that officers should include in all reports?

a. who, what, when, where, why
b. who, what, when, whether, what for
c. who, what, when, why, while
d. who, what, when, why not, what for
e. who, what, when, where, and how come

72. Evaluate the following statements:

1. Official reports should not contain the officer's opinion in the narrative.

2. Facts and assumptions are the same thing and should be included in all reports.

3. One use of reports would be to provide follow-up leads for investigators.

a. all three statements are true
b. only statements 1 & 2 are true
c. only statements 1 & 3 are true
d. only statements 2 & 3 are true
e. all three statements are false

73. Which of the following persons are most likely to read a corrections officer's report?

a. other officers, supervisors, media reporters,

school personnel
b. reporters, supervisors, agencies, maintenance workers
c. other officers, supervisors, lawyers, judges, media representatives
d. informants, suspects, inmates, prisoners
e. criminal justice students, attorneys, jurors, judges

74. It is best to write sentences using _____ voice because they are usually very clear.

a. active
b. passive
c. future tense and active
d. future tense and passive
e. it makes no difference

75. Sentences flow smoothly when ideas are in a consistent format. Which of the following sentences is parallel in construction?

a. Chuck was smoking, drinking, and humming a tune.
b. Pete was dancing, singing a tune, and whistles.
c. Joe likes to bowl, go swimming, and take hikes.
d. Angie likes to type, do filing, and sort papers.
e. none of the above

76. A criminal case in which an arrest has been made should contain which of the following items?

a. an initial investigative report
b. affidavits, if appropriate
c. a witness list
d. a list of officers performing major tasks in the case
e. all of the answers are correct

77. In military time, 1100 would be the same as which of the following times?

a. 1 am
b. 1 pm
c. 11 am
d. 11 pm
e. noon

78. In military time, 2300 would be the same as which of the following times?

a. 1 am
b. 1 pm
c. 11 am
d. 11 pm
e. noon

79. Evaluate the following statements:

1. Agency reports are used for compiling statistical data on victims, suspects, time of occurrence, and day of the week.

2. Sentences often vary in length. Those sentences that contain over 25 words are probably too long and could be made into two or more sentences.

3. It is not necessary to proofread a report before turning it in because that is one of the Sergeant's jobs.

a. all three statements are true
b. only statements 1 & 2 are true
c. only statements 1 & 3 are true
d. only statements 2 & 3 are true
e. all three statements are false

80. Evaluate the following statements:

1. Generally the first officer to arrive on the scene is the person who is responsible for writing the report.

2. Your narrative should contain the facts of the incident and the elements of the charge.

3. Reporting procedures were established to ensure the accuracy and uniformity of reports written by officers.

a. all three statements are true
b. only statements 1 & 2 are true
c. only statements 1 & 3 are true
d. only statements 2 & 3 are true
e. all three statements are false

81. Evaluate the following statements:

1. An officer who has a good memory will not have to make notes on an incident.

2. All reports should be accurate, legible, on time, and written in standard English.

3. Corrections officers should write reports in the first person.

a. all three statements are false
b. only statements 1 & 2 are false
c. only statements 1 & 3 are false
d. only statements 2 & 3 are true
e. all three statements are true

82. Which of the following words is spelled incorrectly?
    a. admnistrative
    b. correctional
    c. confinement
    d. investigator
    e. judicial

83. Which of the following words is spelled incorrectly?
    a. disciplinary
    b. dormitory
    c. cokaine
    d. responsibility
    e. misdemeanor

84. Which of the following words is spelled incorrectly?
    a. marijuana
    b. roster
    c. cercumstance
    d. superintendent
    e. captain

85. Which of the following words is spelled incorrectly?
    a. personel
    b. psychologist
    c. facilitate
    d. autopsy
    e. coroner

86. Which of the following words is spelled incorrectly?
    a. characteristics
    b. hypodermic
    c. sergeant
    d. suspisous
    e. lieutenant

87. Which of the following words is spelled incorrectly?
    a. possession
    b. assault
    c. aggravate
    d. paraphernalia
    e. controband

88. Which of the following words is spelled incorrectly?
    a. voluntary
    b. unauthorized
    c. lieutenant
    d. occupant
    e. beligerent

89. Which of the following words is spelled incorrectly?
    a. intimadate
    b. approximately
    c. personal
    d. agitate
    e. subtantiate

90. Which of the following words is spelled incorrectly?
    a. institution
    b. hostile
    c. disrespect
    d. defendent
    e. admission

91. Which of the following words is spelled incorrectly?
    a. corectional
    b. confinement
    c. investigator
    d. autopsy
    e. vehicular

92. Which of the following words is spelled incorrectly?
    a. possession
    b. contraband
    c. defendent
    d. disciplinary
    e. subpoena

93. Which of the following words is spelled incorrectly?
    a. prosecute
    b. atorney
    c. witness
    d. inmate
    e. victim

94. Which of the following words is spelled incorrectly?
    a. sergeant
    b. facilitate

c. characteristec
d. dormitory
e. voir dire

95. Evaluate the following statements:

1. The quality, legibility, and type of agency reports you write cannot be used as a source for officer evaluations.

2. It is a good idea to use institutional slang and abbreviations when writing a report because it shows that you are a seasoned and experienced corrections officer.

3. All relevant facts should be recorded as soon as they are received.

a. all three statements are false
b. only statements 1 & 2 are false
c. only statements 1 & 3 are false
d. only statements 2 & 3 are false
e. all three statements are true

96. Which of the following statements will NOT appear in a report that is said to be completely factual?

a. "Based on my training and experience ...."
b. "I observed or I saw ...."
c. "The subject was seen ...."
d. "I believe that ...."
e. "Witnesses described the suspect as ...."

97. The phrase "I saw" as opposed to "this officer observed" is an example of which of the following?

a. first person
b. third person
c. active voice
d. second person
e. passive voice

98. Select the sentence which has correct capitalization :

a. Inmate Jones was placed in Jackson Correctional Institute.
b. Inmate Jones was placed in Jackson correctional institute.
c. Inmate Jones was placed in Jackson Correctional facility.
d. Inmate jones was placed in Jackson Correctional Facility.
e. none of the above sentences are correct

99. Which of the following is NOT a reason for reporting procedures?

a. ensure uniformity of documents
b. ensure accuracy of reports
c. ensure compliance with Georgia criminal statutes
d. eliminate errors through consistency
e. help compile data for planning purposes

100. Which of the following lists the basic steps in report writing in the correct order of sequence?

a. gather the facts, organize the facts, evaluate the report
b. gather the facts, record the facts, organize the facts, write the report, evaluate the report
c. gather the facts, record the facts, organize the facts, write the report
d. gather the facts, record the facts, organize the facts, evaluate the report
e. gather the facts, organize the facts, record the facts, write the report, evaluate the report

101. A public record, according to Florida law, includes which of the following items?

a. papers, maps, letters, tapes, other material regardless of physical form
b. papers, maps, books, written material only
c. sound recordings, tapes, videos and all audible materials
d. photographs, crime scene evidence, victim information
e. only minutes of meetings conducted under the "Sunshine Act"

102. Which of the following is NOT a primary duty of the radio communications officer?

a. send messages
b. dispatch units to calls for service
c. maintain up-to-the-minute status of all units
d. receive incoming messages
e. be available to handle calls for service

103. When transmitting a radio message, how should you hold the microphone or portable unit?

a. approximately 1 to 3 inches away from your mouth
b. 12 to 18 inches away from your mouth
c. in the right hand
d. in the left hand
e. none of the above

104. Evaluate the following statements:

1. When talking on the radio, displays of emotion should be avoided.

2. A good working relationship between the officer in the field and the radio communications officer is very important.

3. Generally, official radio communications can be considered "secure" as Florida statutes prohibit civilian personnel from maintaining a law enforcement frequency receiver in a place of business or a vehicle.

a. all three statements are true
b. only statements 1 & 2 are true
c. only statements 1 & 3 are true
d. only statements 2 & 3 are true
e. all three statements are false

105. The primary components of a belt-worn or hand-held portable radio do NOT include which of the following?

a. carrying case
b. transceiver
c. battery
d. remote microphone
e. push-to-talk switch

106. Which of the following types of radio codes do officers rarely use in the field?

a. alpha
b. alpha-numeric
c. numeric
d. Morse code
e. all of the above are commonly used by officers in the field

107. What do the initials FCIC stand for?

a. Federal Communication Information Center
b. Federal Crime Information Center
c. Florida Communication Information Center
d. Florida Criminal Information Center
e. Florida Crime Information Center

108. What does NCIC stand for?

a. National Center for Information Control
b. National Communication Information Center
c. National Crime Information Center
d. Network Communication Information Center
e. Network Criminal Identification Center

109. What does the Florida Crime Information Center provide through its computer network?

a. information on all crimes committed in the state
b. information on the percentage of crimes committed in an area
c. laboratory test results for new law enforcement products
d. criminal history information
e. a list of job vacancies for sworn personnel

110. What does the Florida Crime Information Center NOT provide through its computer network?

a. wanted and missing persons
b. stolen property
c. registered sexual predators
d. daily local weather reports
e. vehicle/vessel identification data

Chapter 5 Answer Key

1. A
2. C
3. C
4. D
5. A
6. A
7. A
8. B
9. D
10. E

11. C
12. C
13. E
14. D
15. C
16. D
17. D
18. E
19. A
20. C

21. D
22. C
23. A
24. A
25. A
26. E
27. A
28. D
29. C
30. A

31. D
32. E
33. A
34. D
35. A
36. E
37. B
38. D
39. C
40. B

41. C
42. A
43. D
44. A
45. A
46. E
47. E
48. E
49. A
50. B

51. D
52. B
53. E
54. C
55. D
56. A
57. B
58. B
59. C
60. E

61. E
62. A
63. D
64. A
65. E
66. C
67. D
68. C
69. E
70. D

71. A
72. C
73. C
74. A
75. A
76. E
77. C
78. D
79. B
80. A

81. D
82. A
83. C
84. C
85. A
86. D
87. E
88. E
89. A
90. D

91. A
92. C
93. B
94. C
95. B
96. D
97. A
98. A
99. C
100. B

101. A
102. E
103. A
104. B
105. A
106. D
107. E
108. C
109. D
110. D

CHAPTER 6

DEFENSIVE TACTICS, WEAPONS, FIRST RESPONDER, AND EMERGENCY PREPAREDNESS

Chapter Overview

As you already know, the role of a corrections officer in today's society encompasses a wide range of activities. This section of your test preparation helps capture that flavor. Just as in previous portions of this guide, the questions that appear in this section were chosen to reflect the goals and objectives that guide the corrections academy training. By the time you complete this section, you should have a firm understanding of the following topics:

- Defensive Tactics
- Use of Force Matrix/Levels of Resistance Matrix
- Prisoner Transport Methods
- Custody Responsibilities/Custody Process Requirements
- Person Search Techniques
- Firearms Safety Procedures
- Ammunition Use
- Service Weapon Use on the Range
- Shotgun Use on the Range
- Chemical Agent Use
- Medical First Responder Techniques
- Riot and Disturbance Control
- Techniques for Handling Unusual Occurrences
- Hostage Procedures
- Emergency Procedures
- Firefighting Principles

Questions

1. Which of the following is NOT a suspect resistance level recognized by the Florida "Use of Force/Levels of Resistance" Matrix?

   a. presence
   b. verbal
   c. active physical
   d. active mental
   e. aggravated physical

2. Which of the following is NOT an officer response level recognized by the Florida "Use of Force/Levels of Resistance" Matrix?

   a. deadly force
   b. taunting a suspect
   c. take downs
   d. restraint devices
   e. dialogue

3. Which of the following subject resistance levels has the potential for deadly force harm to an officer?

   a. presence
   b. aggravated physical
   c. aggressive physical
   d. passive physical
   e. active physical

4. Which level of resistance is it when a subject makes overt, hostile, attacking movements which may cause injury, but are not likely to cause death or great bodily harm to the officer or others?

   a. aggravated physical
   b. aggressive physical
   c. passive physical
   d. active physical
   e. presence

5. Which level of resistance is it when a subject makes physically evasive movements, such as pushing away or not allowing the officer to get close, to defeat an officer's attempt at control?

   a. presence
   b. passive physical
   c. active physical
   d. aggressive physical
   e. aggravated physical

6. According to the Florida "Use of Force/Levels of Resistance" Matrix, how should an officer react when he or she gains subject compliance?

   a. escalate only one more level to gain complete control
   b. de-escalate to the minimum force necessary to control the subject
   c. remain at the same level to gain complete control
   d. de-escalate one level
   e. disengage and assess how the subject reacts

7. Which of the following terms refers to the situation where an officer is speaking to a subject but remains out of the danger zone with the gun or strong side away from the subject?

   a. symbolic assailant
   b. interrogation stance
   c. verbal direction
   d. pain compliance
   e. interview stance

8. A pressure point technique would be an example of which of the following terms?

   a. take down
   b. restraint device
   c. transporter
   d. interview technique
   e. pain compliance

9. Blocking a punch thrown by a suspect would be an example of which of the following terms?

   a. counter move
   b. take down
   c. pain compliance
   d. touch
   e. transporter

10. Cuffing and uncuffing are located at what level of officer response?

    a. one
    b. two
    c. three
    d. four
    e. five

11. Applying leverage to a joint in a technique known as a "bent wrist lock" is a Level Three officer response known as what?

    a. pain compliance
    b. restraint device
    c. transporter
    d. distractive techniques
    e. dialogue

12. According to the Florida Matrix, intermediate weapons constitute which level of officer response?

    a. one
    b. two
    c. three
    d. four
    e. five

13. Which of the following refers to any mechanical tools used to restrict a subject's movement and facilitate search such as handcuffs, flex cuffs, leg irons, or belly chains?

    a. restraint device
    b. transporters
    c. dialogue
    d. take downs
    e. pain compliance

14. Which of the following factors should an officer NOT take into account when making a use of force decision?

    a. number of officers present
    b. available equipment
    c. agency policy
    d. suspect size
    e. suspect race

15. Which of the following verbal and nonverbal cues would suggest the likelihood of an aggressive response from a subject?

    a. abnormal stuttering
    b. rapid and angry movements
    c. increased breathing rate
    d. refusal to show palms of hands
    e. all of the above

16. Evaluate the following statements:

    1. The interview stance is demonstrated by standing directly in front of the subject with the officer's hands behind his or her back so as not to intimidate the subject.

    2. Pain compliance is a Level 5 officer response.

    3. The radial nerve is considered a potential deadly force target.

    a. all three statements are false
    b. only statements 1 & 2 are false
    c. only statements 1 & 3 are false
    d. only statements 2 & 3 are false
    e. all three statements are true

17. What is the proper hand position in the interview stance?

    a. hands by side
    b. chest high with open hands
    c. waist high with open hands
    d. waist high with clenched fists
    e. one hand hidden in a pants pocket

18. What is the proper foot position in the interview stance?

    a. feet together, facing subject
    b. feet apart, facing subject
    c. weak foot forward
    d. strong foot forward
    e. it makes no difference which foot is forward

19. What is the least desirable position from which to approach a subject?

    a. 12 o'clock
    b. 3 o'clock
    c. 4 o'clock
    d. 6 o'clock
    e. 9 o'clock

20. What should an officer always do when confronted with a potentially aggressive situation?

    a. use the target glance
    b. ignore the subject
    c. use profanity to let the subject see the officer is not scared
    d. check first for witnesses who will be favorable to the officer's side
    e. keep the subject's hands in plain view

21. How would a technique that renders a subject temporarily unconscious be classified?

a. intermediate weapon
b. incapacitation technique
c. pain compliance weapon
d. deadly force weapon
e. transporter

22. How are items such as tear gas, straight batons, side handle batons, and flashlights classified?

a. incapacitation weapons
b. pain compliance weapons
c. intermediate weapons
d. deadly force weapons
e. lethal force weapons

23. Ordinarily, which of the following is NOT considered an appropriate pressure point technique?

a. hollow behind ear
b. thumb pressure on the eyeball
c. hollow behind collarbone
d. under jaw
e. base of biceps

24. The major parts of handcuffs do NOT include which of the following?

a. carrying case
b. swivel eye
c. ratchet
d. frame
e. chain links or hinges

25. Except in emergency situations, handcuffs that are placed on a suspect will always be secured in which fashion?

a. single locked
b. double locked
c. triple locked
c. auto locked
d. unlocked

26. Evaluate the following statements:

1. Fluid shock wave involves striking a muscle mass and letting it "sink in."

2. A common peroneal knee spike is always considered a distraction technique.

3. When an officer is trying to escape from a front or rear choke, it is best to use slow deliberate movements to insure the technique is done properly.

a. all three statements are false
b. only statements 1 & 2 are false
c. only statements 1 & 3 are false
d. only statements 2 & 3 are false
e. all three statements are true

27. When confronted with resistance, at what point does an officer have the option to escalate or disengage?

a. point of initial contact only
b. point of aggressive physical resistance only
c. any point
d. at no point is this an option
e. either a or b only

28. What must the officer do as soon as the point of subject compliance is reached?

a. notify a supervisor
b. fill out a use of force report
c. de-escalate the response level to the minimum force with which the responding officer is proficient
d. de-escalate the response level ONLY if an incapacitating technique has been used
e. de-escalate the response level to the minimum force necessary to control the subject

29. What is the purpose behind searching a suspect?

a. officer safety
b. discovery of weapons
c. discovery of contraband or evidence
d. safety of officers in the vicinity of the suspect
e. all of the above

30. Evaluate the following statements:

1. Using seriousness of the current crime as an indicator of the potential threat that the suspect poses is a mistake officers should avoid when transporting a prisoner.

2. After a police officer brings an arrested person to the county jail, the arrested person needs to be searched only if the police officer says that he or she did not conduct a search already.

3. The head is considered a potential deadly force target.

a. all three statements are true
b. only statements 1 & 2 are true
c. only statements 1 & 3 are true
d. only statements 2 & 3 are true
e. all three statements are false

31. Which of the following is NOT an element of safe prisoner transport?

a. an adequate number of personnel
b. vehicle used for transport is properly equipped and in good working order
c. seat belts for the prisoner
d. following agency guidelines
e. all of the above

32. Which of the following is NOT a reason for searching and restraining a prisoner prior to transport?

a. prevent escapes
b. officer safety
c. prisoner safety
d. confiscate any potential weapons
e. to check for any possible evidence

33. Evaluate the following statements:

1. It is necessary to search a transport vehicle for possible contraband before transporting a prisoner.

2. One basic mistake that officers should avoid in prisoner transports is wasting time in the transport process.

3. It is necessary to search a transport vehicle for possible contraband after transporting a prisoner.

a. all three statements are true
b. only statements 1 & 2 are true
c. only statements 1 & 3 are true
d. only statements 2 & 3 are true
e. all three statements are false

34. Which of the following categories of personnel does NOT have the authority to confine a prisoner to the jail?

a. local law enforcement officers
b. state law enforcement officers
c. a loss prevention employee of a department store
d. parole and probation officers
e. federal law enforcement officers

35. Which of the following is NOT an admission requirement for accepting an individual for confinement in a jail?

a. proper identification of the person delivering the prisoner
b. proper identification of the prisoner being delivered
c. completing the appropriate admission forms
d. obtaining proper legal papers giving authority for commitment or detention
e. none of the above

36. Evaluate the following statements pertaining to custody classification and housing assignments:

1. Violent, aggressive prisoners should be housed alone.

2. Handicapped, sick, or injured prisoners should be housed in an area where medical services are readily available.

3. Prisoners believed to be under the influence of drugs or alcohol should be monitored and observed.

a. all three statements are true
b. only statements 1 & 2 are true
c. only statements 1 & 3 are true
d. only statements 2 & 3 are true
e. all three statements are false

37. Which of the following terms refers to a cursory search for weapons and contraband large enough to be detected through clothing?

a. strip search
b. clothed search
c. stop-and-frisk procedure
d. noninvasive technique
e. body cavity search

38. Which of the following personnel can conduct a body cavity search?

a. the immediate supervisor
b. any corrections officer
c. physician or designated health personnel
d. the highest ranking officer on duty
e. any intake personnel

39. Which of the following is NOT an element of a successful inmate search?

a. systematic
b. performed in an orderly fashion
c. conducted in the presence of other inmates
d. done with care and attention on the part of the searching officer
e. thorough

40. Evaluate the following statements:

1. During a clothed search, the officer should reach into the inmate's pockets to check for weapons or contraband.

2. The officer should run his or her hands through the inmate's hair to check for weapons or contraband.

3. When conducting a clothed search, the officer should pay special attention to collars, cuffs, belts, waistbands, and seams.

a. all three statements are false
b. only statements 1 & 2 are false
c. only statements 1 & 3 are false
d. only statements 2 & 3 are false
e. all three statements are true

41. When is it advisable to conduct a strip search of an inmate?

a. before an escape attempt
b. when re-entering the institution after being outside for work or some other activity
c. prior to a contact visit
d. upon the request of the arresting law enforcement officer
e. under none of these conditions

42. Evaluate the following statements:

1. Firearms stored at home should be unloaded and locked away from children.

2. Most handgun cartridges have the potential to penetrate doors and interior walls of typical residential construction, and may overpenetrate a human target.

3. While on duty, you should unsnap your holster so that your weapon is ready for immediate use if you are responding to a potentially dangerous situation.

a. all three statements are true
b. only statements 1 & 2 are true
c. only statements 1 & 3 are true
d. only statements 2 & 3 are true
e. all three statements are false

43. Which of the following is NOT a component of a firearm cartridge?

a. ejector
b. case
c. primer
d. bullet/projectiles
e. powder

44. What is the purpose of the primer in the center fire?

a. to provide recoil for shooter feedback
b. to project the bullet out of the barrel
c. to expand the shell casing against the chamber
d. to ignite the powder in the shell
e. both b & d above

45. The most commonly used handgun ammunition for law enforcement and corrections duty use include which of the following?

a. jacketed hollow point/controlled expansion
b. lead semi-wadcutter
c. copper coated semi-wadcutter
d. Glasser safety slug
e. lead square nose

46. Which of the following represents the most commonly used shotgun ammunition?

a. blanks
b. rifled shotshell
c. trial loads
d. buckshot
e. none of the above

47. It is possible and safe to shoot .38 ammunition in which of the following weapons?

a. .25 semi-auto pistol
b. .40 revolver
c. .357 revolver
d. 10 mm semi-auto pistol
e. 9 mm semi-auto pistol

48. What should a person do immediately upon picking up a revolver?

a. pull the trigger to see if the weapon is loaded
b. be sure the safety is on and the action open
c. look down the bore for any possible obstructions
d. pointing the weapon in a safe direction, open the cylinder to see that it is unloaded
e. pointing the weapon in a safe direction, remove the magazine, lock the slide back, and look to see that the revolver is unloaded

49. Where should the trigger finger be when drawing a handgun from the holster?

a. outside the trigger guard
b. inside the trigger guard but off the trigger

c. inside the trigger but maintaining light pressure on the trigger
d. on the safety
e. on the hammer

50. Before shooting a firearm, it is an officer's responsibility to:

a. positively identify the target
b. know the capabilities of his or her ammunition
c. know what or who is beyond the target
d. all of the above
e. a & c above only

51. If a shooter has a malfunction, such as a misfire, while on the line during firearms training, he or she should:

1. raise the non-shooting hand to signal the range officer

2. keep the firearm pointed downrange

3. raise the shooting hand to signal the range officer

4. keep the firearm pointed up in the air

5. holster the weapon safely and raise a hand to signal the range officer

6. have the weapon inspected by a certified range officer

a. statements 1, 2, & 6 are correct
b. statements 1, 4, & 6 are correct
c. statements 5 & 6 are correct
d. statements 2, 3, & 6 are correct
e. statements 3, 4, & 6 are correct

52. What usually happens with a squib load?

a. a projectile lodges or is suspected to be lodged in an auto magazine
b. a projectile lodges or is suspected to be lodged in the cylinder or bore
c. a projectile lodges or is suspected to be jammed by the ejector
d. a projectile lodges or is suspected to be jammed by the extractor
e. nothing except that the bullet travels down range at a much lower rate of speed and experiences a considerable drop due to gravity

53. Which of the following is NOT a major part of a revolver?

a. magazine
b. trigger
c. hammer
d. ejector rod
e. cylinder release

54. Which of the following is NOT a major part of a semi-auto pistol?

a. slide
b. trigger
c. safety
d. ejector rod
e. magazine

55. Which of the following steps is INCORRECT in safely drawing a handgun from a holster?

a. unsnap retention device
b. grasp stock or grips with the finger outside the trigger guard
c. grasp stock or grips with the finger inside the trigger guard
d. pull from the holster
e. move the muzzle by the most direct route in the direction of target

56. Which of the following positions is NOT used when firing a service handgun?

a. high ready position
b. low ready position
c. kneeling-low point
d. prone
e. lying on the back

57. What is the purpose for maintaining a firearm in the ready position?

a. to be prepared to quickly engage a deadly threat or suspected deadly threat
b. allow the officer a wide field of view without maintaining tunnel vision
c. to avoid tiring out the officer from unnecessary reholstering
d. it makes reloading much quicker and safer
e. both a & b

58. What is the first thing a person should do upon picking up a semi-auto pistol?

a. pull the trigger to see if the weapon is loaded
b. be sure the safety is on and the action is open
c. point the weapon in a safe direction, put safety on, remove the magazine, and lock the slide back to ensure that it is unloaded

d. point the weapon in a safe direction, open the cylinder to see that it is unloaded
e. look down the bore for any possible obstructions

59. What does sight alignment include?

a. front sight aligned with rear sight, focus on front sight, importance of using both eyes in sighting
b. front sight aligned with rear sight, focus on rear sight, importance of strong eye use in sighting
c. front sight aligned with rear sight, focus on front sight, importance of strong eye use in sighting
d. muzzle aligned with front sight, focus on rear sight, importance of weak eye use in sighting
e. focus on front sight only

60. Which of the following safety steps should a person NOT take immediately upon picking up a pump shotgun?

a. pull the trigger to see if the weapon is loaded
b. be sure the safety is on
c. elevate the muzzle
d. open the action
e. keep weapon pointed in a safe direction

61. Which of the following is NOT a proper procedure for unloading and reloading a service revolver while maintaining an awareness of the target?

a. keep muzzle pointed towards target
b. utilize cover if available
c. attempt to catch expended casings
d. resume the position of covering the target after reloading is completed
e. all are acceptable procedures

62. Which of the following is NOT one of the major parts of a shotgun?

a. stock
b. load port
c. ejection port
d. safety
e. front and rear sights

63. What are the safety checks that one should perform on a shotgun?

a. engage safety
b. unload without chambering rounds in and out of action
c. visually inspect chamber, magazine, and bore
d. maintain muzzle in a safe direction
e. all of the above

64. Which of the following is NOT a proper procedure when loading a shotgun?

a. elevate muzzle and point in a safe direction
b. put the safety on
c. load shells into the loading port
d. make sure the slide is back and safety is off
e. make sure the shells are pushed far enough into the magazine that shell latches engage

65. The shotgun is considered to be what kind of a bore weapon?

a. rifled
b. clean
c. smooth
d. landed
e. grooved

66. How many pellets does a 12 gauge "00" buckshot standard load 2 3/4-inch shotshell contain?

a. 3
b. 5
c. 7
d. 9
e. 15

67. Which of the following is NOT part of the proper position for firing a shotgun?

a. put support hand in place
b. place the muzzle next to one's cheek
c. assume a kneeling or standing position
d. put heel of stock against the shoulder
e. position feet to steady oneself

68. Aiming a shotgun requires which of the following considerations?

a. sighting
b. point of aim
c. considering the effect of distance on trajectory
d. considering the effect of distance on shot pattern
e. all of the above

69. What should be the first reaction of an officer coming under a deadly threat?

a. draw a service weapon and prepare to return fire

b. attempt to distract the person making the threat by placing his or her hand on the butt of the holstered service weapon
c. move to cover or concealment while drawing the firearm
d. advise headquarters of the need for assistance
e. invoke crisis reaction techniques by speaking softly, but firmly, to the assailant

70. Which of the following can result from a chemical agent?

a. smoke screen
b. incendiary action
c. toxic effect
d. inflammatory reaction
e. all of the above

71. Which of the following refers to an irritant or a harassing agent?

a. a known antidote usually does not exist
b. capable of killing upon contact with the skin
c. capable of killing if decontamination does not begin immediately
d. capable of killing if inhaled
e. not sufficiently toxic to cause death

72. The amount of chemical present in a unit volume of air at any one time defines which of the following terms?

a. concentration
b. dispersion
c. toxicity
d. accelerant
e. propellant

73. Which of the following terms best describes a vapor?

a. a liquid
b. a gas
c. a solid form
d. smoke
e. none of the above

74. An aerosol spray is a mixture of what?

a. a liquid and an accelerant
b. a gas and an accelerant
c. a solid and a propellant
d. a liquid and a propellant
e. none of the above

75. Which of the following is NOT one of the four primary types of chemical agents used in law enforcement and corrections?

a. CN chemical agent
b. CS chemical agent
c. HC (smoke)
d. OC derivatives
e. percussion grenade

76. Which of the following parts of the human body is usually not affected by CN and CS exposure?

a. eyes
b. nose
c. skin
d. ears
e. lungs

77. Which of the following does NOT describe a proper first-aid procedure for treating exposure to CN or CS agents?

a. remove victim from contaminated area
b. flush out any particles in the eyes with cool water
c. flush contaminated skin areas with water
d. flush contaminated skin areas with rubbing alcohol
e. contact a physician

78. What are the basic methods for disseminating chemical agents?

a. burning, fog, liquid, aerosol
b. blast, projection, fog, liquid, aerosol
c. blast, burning, fog, liquid, aerosol
d. blast, burning, fog, spray, aerosol
e. fog, liquid, aerosol

79. Which of the following is NOT a proper deployment system of chemical agents?

a. shotgun round
b. canisters
c. pepper fogger
d. aerosol
e. all are proper deployment systems

80. Which of the following factors does NOT influence the effectiveness of chemical agents?
a. wind direction
b. wind speed
c. time of day, specifically night versus day
d. humidity

e. characteristics of the target

81. Which of the following is NOT a proper procedure when using an aerosol chemical weapon?

a. do not use within two feet of the target person
b. do not spray into the wind
c. aim at the chest and chin areas of the target person
d. aim at the feet of the target person
e. all are acceptable procedures

82. Which of the following should NOT be done when putting on a gas mask?

a. remove mask from carrying case
b. place chin into mask and pull webbing over head
c. check the mask for a proper seal
d. spray a minute amount of the chemical agent into the mask so the wearer will acclimate to it
e. adjust straps for tighter fit

83. What are some disadvantages to wearing a gas mask?

a. increases breathing ability, speaking ability, and field of vision
b. impedes speaking ability, field of vision, and shouldering a firearm
c. impedes speaking ability, field of vision, and facial blood system
d. impedes speaking ability, field of vision, hearing
e. impedes speaking ability, movement, and hearing

84. Officer Gibbons is dispatched to an accident with injuries in the shop area. Upon arrival, Officer Gibbons is greeted with the following conditions:

1. Inmate #1 has a broken arm.

2. Inmate #2 has a nose bleed and a possible broken nose.

3. Inmate #3 has a number of superficial wounds and is bleeding from the face.

4. Inmate #4 is unconscious, but is still breathing.

5. Inmate #5 has no pulse and no respiration.

Which one of these persons should Officer Gibbons tend to first?

a. Inmate #1
b. Inmate #2
c. Inmate #3
d. Inmate #4
e. Inmate #5

85. Which of the following actions is NOT a major role or responsibility of the medical first responder?

a. gaining access to the patient using simple tools
b. interviewing witnesses to determine what has happened
c. providing emergency care with minimal equipment
d. lifting and moving the patient if such movement is required
e. none of the above

86. Which of the following is NOT one of the major body components?

a. skull
b. fingers
c. spinal column
d. thorax
e. pelvic cavity

87. Which of the following pair of terms does NOT belong on this list?

a. superficial/deep
b. medial/lateral
c. head/feet
d. superior/inferior
e. anterior/posterior

88. Which of the following terms does NOT belong to the respiratory system?

a. appendix
b. pharynx
c. trachea
d. lungs
e. diaphragm and rib muscles

89. Which of the following can be a sign of adequate or inadequate breathing?

a. rise and fall of chest
b. hearing air being expelled from the mouth
c. cyanosis
d. noisy breathing
e. all of the above are signs

90. Which of the following is NOT one of the three techniques for maintaining an open airway for adults?

a. head tilt-chin lift
b. jaw-thrust
c. modified jaw-thrust without head tilt
d. closed jaw vertical position
e. all of the above are basic techniques

91. Which of the following terms refers to a person who wears a surgically inserted neck breather?

a. pharyngectomee
b. pleuryngectomee
c. laryngectomee
d. diaphragmnectomee
e. epiglottyngectomee

92. Which of the following is NOT a sign of cardiac arrest?

a. patient is not breathing
b. patient has no carotid pulse
c. no brachial pulse for an infant
d. cannot hear any air from mouth
e. all of the above are signs of cardiac arrest

93. Which of the following is NOT a sign of effective CPR?

a. carotid/brachial pulse is felt
b. improved skin color
c. pupils may react when exposed to light
d. carotid pulse is absent
e. heart resumes beating

94. Which of the following complications may occur if CPR is performed incorrectly?

a. perforated ear drum
b. broken ribs
c. chipped tooth
d. collapsed nasal passage
e. broken arm

95. Which of the following terms does NOT refer to a type of artery?

a. radial
b. carotid
c. femoral
d. superficial
e. all of the above refer to a type

96. The failure of the circulatory system to provide sufficient circulation to every body part describes which of the following medical terms?

a. shock
b. cyanosis
c. trauma
d. bleeding
e. renal failure

97. Which of the following signs or symptoms is NOT associated with shock?

a. profuse sweating
b. weak and rapid pulse
c. cold and clammy skin
d. bleeding from the ears
e. fainting

98. Which of the following terms refers to an acute allergic reaction?

a. ancillary shock
b. anaphylactic shock
c. renal shock
d. cardiopulmonary shock
e. myalgia

99. Which of the following techniques should be used as a last resort for control of bleeding in an extremity?

a. tourniquet
b. elevation
c. pressure point
d. direct pressure
e. none of the above

100. Which of the following terms applies to the situation where there is a broken bone protruding through the skin?

a. separation
b. dislocation
c. simple fracture
d. compound fracture
e. avulsion

101. Which of the following is NOT a general rule for splinting?

a. cover all wounds with sterile dressing
b. immobilize the joint above and below fracture or dislocation
c. reset any protruding bones before splinting

d. splint all fractures before moving patient
e. splint dislocations in position found

102. Whenever the heart is not getting enough oxygen, the body experiences pain. Which of the following terms refers to that condition?

a. heart systole
b. heart failure
c. stroke
d. shock
e. angina

103. Which of the following terms best describes the condition when the heart is not pumping blood efficiently to the rest of the body, fresh blood cannot enter the heart from the lungs, and blood and other fluids are accumulating in the body?

a. heart systole
b. heart failure
c. stroke
d. shock
e. angina

104. Typically, how long can human brain cells survive without oxygen?

a. 1-2 minutes
b. 2-4 minutes
c. 4-6 minutes
d. 6-8 minutes
e. 8-10 minutes

105. Which of the following reasons best describes why a first responder would splint a dislocated joint prior to transporting an injured person?

a. shorten angle
b. prevent comminution
c. protect the separation
d. prevent motion
e. to ease the patient's pain

106. Which of the following refers to a "breech birth?"

a. a birth in which the hands appear first
b. a birth that occurs when the mother cannot get to the hospital in time
c. a birth in which the head is presented first
d. a birth in which the feet and head are presented first
e. a birth in which the buttocks or feet are presented first

107. In terms of childbirth, a "prolapsed cord" refers to which of the following?

a. condition of birth in which the umbilical cord has come out of the vagina before the baby is born
b. condition of birth in which the umbilical cord has come out of the cervix before the baby is born
c. condition of birth in which the skin accordia pro lapsis birth attachments has come out of the vagina before the baby is born
d. condition of birth in which the umbilical cord has come out of the amniotic sac
e. condition of birth in which the umbilical cord is wrapped around the baby's neck

108. Cervical collars are used to protect which portion of the body?

a. arms and shoulders
b. cranium
c. knee and lower leg
d. pelvic area
e. neck and spine

109. For triage purposes, which of the following conditions has the highest priority?

a. cardiac arrest
b. burns
c. back injury
d. fractured arm
e. death

110. Which of the following is NOT a major communicable disease among adults?

a. arteriosclerosis
b. tuberculosis
c. hepatitis
d. syphilis
e. chlamydia

111. Which of the following precautions should be taken to avoid contracting communicable diseases?

a. use a mask with a one-way valve when administering CPR
b. wear disposable latex gloves

c. wash hands frequently and thoroughly
d. use goggles or safety glasses when there is the possibility of handling body fluids
e. all of the above

112. Officer Nichols has a prisoner who complains that he feels very tired, weak, and is running a fever. The prisoner also has a terrible cough and spits up blood every time he coughs. These symptoms describe which of the following communicable diseases?

a. gonorrhea
b. hepatitis A
c. hepatitis B
d. AIDS
e. tuberculosis

113. Evaluate the following statements:

1. The most common method of transmission for tuberculosis is airborne transmission through close contact.

2. Yellowing of the skin and eyes is associated with hepatitis.

3. AIDS can be transmitted from germs on toilet seats.

a. all three statements are true
b. only statements 1 & 2 are true
c. only statements 1 & 3 are true
d. only statements 2 & 3 are true
e. all three statements are false

114. Officer Bivens is monitoring inmates who are playing basketball. Suddenly, one prisoner who is sixty years old stands still for a moment, clutches his chest, and falls to the floor. Which of the following conditions match these symptoms?

a. heart attack
b. asthma
c. stroke
d. diabetic coma
e. insulin shock

115. The phrase "an uncontrolled, violent disturbance undertaken by inmates in a correctional setting, usually directed at the central administration of the correctional facility" best fits which of the following terms?

a. argument
b. riot
c. insurrection
d. grievance
e. task force

116. Which of the following is NOT a typical causal factor for riots and disturbances inside correctional facilities?

a. food
b. mail
c. humanity
d. low staff morale
e. medical treatment

117. Which of the following is NOT an indicator of facility tension that often precedes a riot or disturbance?

a. increased number of requests for transfers
b. increase in recreational activities
c. discovery of more weapons during shakedowns
d. increased separation by racial or ethnic groups
e. warnings to "friendly" officers to be careful

118. Evaluate the following statements:

1. A inmate disturbance may be used as a diversion for an escape attempt.

2. The purpose of a riot and disorder plan is to nip these occurrences in the bud before they materialize.

3. The best thing for a corrections officer to do if taken hostage during a disturbance within a correctional facility is to give up his or her uniform immediately.

a. all three statements are false
b. only statements 1 & 2 are false
c. only statements 1 & 3 are false
d. only statements 2 & 3 are false
e. all three statements are true

119. Evaluate the following statements:

1. The major responsibility of a correctional officer who discovers a disturbance in progress is to allow himself or herself to be taken hostage so the administration has a trusted person on the inside.

2. The initial steps for an officer to take upon discovering a disturbance in progress are to notify central communications of the situation and to secure the area.

3. The officer discovering a disturbance in progress should attempt to establish a dialogue with the leaders so as to quell the uprising as quickly as possible.

a. all three statements are true
b. only statements 1 & 2 are true
c. only statements 1 & 3 are true
d. only statements 2 & 3 are true
e. all three statements are false

120. Which of the following reflects the appropriate priorities from highest to lowest when dealing with a riot in a correctional facility?

a. protection of property, safety of inmates, safety of hostages
b. protection of general public, safety of hostages, safety of staff
c. restoration of control, protection of property, safety of hostages
d. identification of dissidents, protection of property, safety of hostages
e. protection of property, safety of general public, restoration of control

121. Evaluate the following statements:

1. A general guideline for riot or disturbance situations is that all personnel, whether trained or not, should be provided with firearms for their personal protection.

2. Post-riot procedures should include a strip search of just the known ringleaders and agitators.

3. In the event of an escape, perform a complete lock-down of the inmate population.

a. all three statements are false
b. only statements 1 & 2 are false
c. only statements 1 & 3 are false
d. only statements 2 & 3 are false
e. all three statements are true

122. Which of the following is NOT an appropriate procedure to follow when responding to an inmate death ?

a. verify apparent death and notify the supervisor
b. summon medical personnel and secure the area
c. notify the chaplain and hospital social worker of the death
d. immediately notify the inmate's family of the incident
e. prepare a report containing all known facts related to the death

123. The four components of a fire include heat, fuel, oxygen, and what else?

a. combustion
b. chemical chain reaction
c. light
d. smoke
e. time

124. What class of fire includes electrical components?

a. Class A
b. Class B
c. Class C
d. Class D
e. Class E

125. What should an officer be aware of when he or she responds to a Class B fire call?

a. the fire involves combustible metals
b. the fire involves rubber material
c. the fire involves flammable liquids
d. the fire is electrical
e. all of the above

126. What is a safety precaution to use when operating a portable water fire extinguisher?

a. do not use water on a Class A fire
b. do not use water on a Class B fire
c. water should only be used on a Class B fire
d. water should only be used on a Class C fire
e. water should only be used on a Class E fire

127. What is the primary purpose of a fire rescue operation?

a. containment
b. preserve life
c. fire prevention
d. redirection
e. on-the-job training

128. The basic procedures for using a portable fire extinguisher are known as PASS. What do these initials stand for?

a. pull pin, aim nozzle, squeeze handles, sweep at the base of the flame
b. pull fire alarm, alert people inside, safely escort them outside, spray the fire
c. pull pin, approach the fire safely, and douse the flames
d. pull pin, activate 911 system, squeeze handles, safely escort people outside
e. pull pin, activate 911 system, safely escort people outside, shut down the area

Chapter 6 Answer Key

1. D
2. B
3. B
4. B
5. C
6. B
7. E
8. E
9. A
10. C

11. C
12. D
13. A
14. E
15. E
16. A
17. C
18. C
19. A
20. E

21. B
22. C
23. B
24. A
25. B
26. D
27. C
28. E
29. E
30. C

31. E
32. C
33. A
34. C
35. B
36. A
37. B
38. C
39. C
40. B

41. B
42. B
43. A
44. D
45. A
46. D
47. C
48. D
49. A
50. D

51. A
52. B
53. A
54. D
55. C
56. E
57. E
58. C
59. C
60. A

61. C
62. E
63. E
64. D
65. C
66. D
67. B
68. E
69. C
70. E

71. E
72. A
73. B
74. D
75. E
76. D
77. D
78. C
79. E
80. C

81. D
82. D
83. B
84. E
85. B
86. B
87. C
88. A
89. E
90. D

91. C
92. E
93. D
94. B
95. D
96. A
97. D
98. B
99. A
100. D

101. C
102. E
103. B
104. C
105. D
106. E
107. A
108. E
109. A
110. A

111. E
112. E
113. B
114. A
115. B
116. C
117. B
118. D
119. D
120. B

121. B
122. D
123. B
124. C
125. C
126. B
127. B
128. A

CHAPTER 7

LAUNCHING THE JOB SEARCH

Introduction

Congratulations! You finally got the certification exam behind you. Now all that is left is to land a corrections job and start that career. But first, how does one find out which agencies are hiring? Then what happens? How do agencies process applications and what kind of hurdles should an applicant expect?

This chapter will guide you through the steps involved in the typical corrections officer selection process and offer some pointers to make you more competitive. What we will do here is talk about job leads, the application, the written test, the background investigation, the medical check, polygraph testing, the psychological interview, and the oral interview.

Who's Hiring?

The first step in the job hunt is to find out what vacancies exist. The most common recruiting method that agencies use is to advertise these openings in the media. Check the want ads in the Sunday newspaper. If you do not subscribe to the major newspaper in your locale or if you are interested in vacancies in other geographical areas, head to the local library. Most public libraries, and even some college libraries, subscribe to newspapers from around the state and house them in a reading room.

While the library approach is straightforward, most people cannot afford to sit around for six days to see if any job openings develop in the Sunday paper. A more active strategy, though, would mean that *you* initiate the contact. Sometimes recruiters will call the corrections academies or mail them information about openings and upcoming jobs. Get in touch with the training facility you attended and ask about any job prospects that may have come in since you graduated. If you went to college, contact the career services office on the campus. See if they have any leads you can follow. Perhaps, they might even have a list of alumni who are currently employed in the corrections sector. If you do not ask, you will never know.

Quite often, people decide that they would like to live in a particular area of the state or that they may wish to remain close to home or to a loved one. Get out a Florida map and, if distance is an important factor in your consideration, determine how far away you would be willing to relocate. Draw a circle around that area and make a list of all the cities and counties within that vicinity. Use the information contained in the appendices to make a telephone call, send a letter of inquiry, or visit the personnel office in these agencies.

What should you do if you feel like you are striking out and not finding any job openings? First of all, you must realize that many agencies take six months or so to process an application for a full-time position. Some agencies, though, have a complement of part-time opportunities. While these spots are restricted to part-time status, they do carry several benefits. For one thing, your state certification is valid for three years. Should you not become gainfully employed by a correctional agency within three years of passing the certification exam, your corrections officer license automatically expires. Working in even a part-time position puts you into the correc-

A Sample Letter of Inquiry

December 1, 1997

Officer Michael G. Williams
Personnel Section
Any Correctional Facility
1234 Main Street
Anywhere, FL 12345

Dear Officer Williams:

I am interested in obtaining an entry-level corrections officer position with your agency.

My background includes graduation from the Florida State University last year with a Bachelor's degree in Criminology and Criminal Justice. After finishing college, I completed the Basic Recruit Curriculum at the Pat Thomas Criminal Justice Training Academy and successfully passed the Florida Corrections Officer Certification Examination. Now I am in the process of seeking full-time employment as a corrections officer.

I would appreciate it if you would forward application materials to me at the following address:

789 Central Avenue
Cityville, FL 98765

Should the need arise, I can be reached at (123) 385-5678.

Thank you.

Sincerely,

Peter K. Rabbit

tions gainfully employed category and stops the three-year clock from ticking down on you.

There are other hidden advantages to accepting a part-time status while waiting for a regular offer of employment. Some agencies will require that you complete an extensive in-house training period before you go out and work in a correctional officer capacity. This procedure allows you to gain more expertise and to compile a relevant corrections work history. Since some agencies hire directly from their in-house part-time employees, you are already a known commodity and may have a distinct advantage over nonsworn candidates who have not worked a single day for any agency.

In any event, whether you accept a part-time position or not, the first task is to submit a written application. The next section addresses that topic.

Minimum Entrance Requirements for Corrections Officers in Florida

To become a corrections officer in the State of Florida, a person must satisfy the following minimum entrance requirements:

- be at least nineteen years old
- be a United States citizen
- hold a high school diploma or its equivalent
- hold an honorable discharge if a previous member of the armed forces
- pass a fingerprint check for a criminal history
- not have any prior felony convictions
- not have any prior misdemeanor convictions involving moral turpitude
- be of good moral character
- successfully complete a basic corrections officer training course
- successfully complete the state corrections officer

The Written Application

You must hand in a written application in order to receive any consideration for a sworn position. The written application is important in several respects. First, the agency will use this information to verify that you do meet the minimum entrance requirements imposed by the state. You will be asked to provide information regarding your citizenship, age, educational attainment, military records, driving background, social security number, criminal involvement, medical history, academy training, certification exam results, and other pertinent areas.

Bear in mind that the typical corrections hiring process utilizes a "weeding out" framework rather than a "screening in" view. In other words, the number of applicants is so large that agencies have the luxury of rejecting applicants for minor transgressions without depleting or seriously compromising the eligibility pool. Thus, some agencies may be able to reject applicants who were ticketed for a moving traffic violation in the past two or three years.

Your goal, of course, is to not be weeded out so you can remain in the candidate pool. What can you do at this point to maximize your chances of remaining eligible? The first thing to do is to make multiple xeroxes of the blank application. Take a practice copy and fill it out by hand. Set the application aside for a day or so and then edit your responses. When you are satisfied with the product, go ahead and type out your responses to the questions. Use correction fluid if you detect any misspellings or other errors. When you finish filling in all the information neatly, make several photocopies of the completed application. Pass out copies to several people for a critical evaluation. Ask them what else they think should go into this document. Review these comments, make changes where appropriate, and go to final copy.

Before you turn in this final copy of your application, reread it to ensure that you have followed all the instructions in full. Some agencies may ask you to fill out a biographical sketch in your own handwriting to see if you write legibly. Do it or else you will risk having your paperwork landing in the "weed out" pile. Also, check any supporting documents to make sure they appear in the proper order. When you are satisfied that the application represents your best possible work, make a photocopy for your records before turning these materials in to the agency. If possible, deliver the application yourself to the agency. If that is not feasible, mail the material first-class with a request for a return-receipt so you will know that the agency has received your package. Otherwise, you will never know if your application made it to the agency. Given all the time and energy you have expended on this project, why take that chance?

Knowing how agencies operate, some job-seekers may be tempted to cut corners during the application process. A simple word of advice is "Don't!" Some people may wonder what should I do about the traffic tickets on my record? Should I hide the mischief and police contact I had when I was a juvenile? What about my work history or the lack of it? What revelations should I make or not make?

The best rule of thumb is to be completely honest and up front with any less than stellar information. If your responses at this stage disqualify you from further consideration, so be it. If you hide something and it surfaces later, say three or four years down the road, your lack of disclosure could be quite embarrassing and often fatal to your career aspirations. The agency will have no choice except to terminate you for submitting a fraudulent employment application. At that point in your career, the prospects of getting hired by another agency that is willing to overlook this tarnish will shrink considerably.

This advice does not mean that you cannot take an adverse circumstance and turn it to your advantage. Someone, for instance, might be embarrassed by the driving record compiled as a teenager. Suppose, for example, you received two citations for reckless driving when you were seventeen years old. Since then, you have been a model citizen, held several jobs, graduated from high school, went on to college, earned acceptable grades, and graduated. During the interim, you maintained a spotless driving record. Attach a neatly typed addendum to your application that outlines what achievements you have accrued since that time and explain how you are a different person today than when you were younger. Also point out that since your license was restored, you learned a hard lesson and your driving has remained impeccable since that time.

Retain a photocopy of the completed application in its entirety for your records. Having this information will make it easier for you to fill out applications to other agencies especially if some of the questions are the same. Should agency personnel misfile your application, it will be easy for you to send another. Furthermore, should somebody question you about your response to a particular inquiry, you will have the exact text in front of you and can see just what this person is referencing.

Once your application is received, office workers will match your information against the state's minimum entrance requirements. If you do not satisfy these standards, the agency will discard you from further consideration. If you meet all these criteria, the next step is to match you up against the agency's minimum entrance qualifications. For example, some agencies may mandate that successful applicants hold a college degree prior to hiring. (The application packet usually contains a list of such requirements.) If a review of your application contains evidence supporting your achievement in this area in the form of a college transcript and a diploma, you receive a green light and will be ushered into the "still eligible" candidate pool.

The Written Examination

Prospective employees who survive the initial cut may be invited to take a written exam. Depending upon the agency, this test may be either an aptitude test or a paper-and-pencil psychological inventory. There is an ample body of research which shows that how well a person does on preservice psychological testing has no bearing on future job performance. But, then, that is not what agencies are attempting to accomplish at this juncture. Public service agencies, especially in the corrections sector, are concerned with reducing their civil liability whenever possible. Making sure that a person is psychologically fit for duty is just one small, but tremendously important, mechanism to ensure that the agency is earning public trust and keeping misfits out of uniform.

There is no way to study for this type of an assessment. The best preparation is to get a good night's sleep before the testing, eat well, and answer the questions to the best of your ability. Most of these tests are arranged so that any cheating or deception will surface during the statistical analysis. The only advice here is to be yourself.

The Background Investigation

Survivors of the selection process are now subject to the background check. The information you provided on the written application is the starting point for this line of inquiry. Investigators will run a credit check, verify your educational degrees, and contact your list of references. The investigation, of course, does not stop here. Everybody knows that applicants only use references who will give very favorable recommendations. Investigators contact these people to establish leads. They may unearth former classmates and seek their opinion of your character. Next-door neighbors usually are in a unique position to provide interesting tidbits about you and your family. Academy instructors will receive a visit and your training records will be open to perusal. In short, the agency wants to make sure that you are an upstanding person and that there are no character flaws in your background that would preclude you from active employment.

The Medical Check

Once the investigators are satisfied that you are a viable candidate, you will be told to schedule a visit to the agency's physician for a physical. Corrections work, as you know, can be quite demanding. Shift work, the abrupt way in which officers sometimes must spring into action, the exertion, and the constant element of danger are all formidable stressors. Physical fitness is an important component of your occupational readiness since it is a solid defense against the ravages of stress. Because stress can aggravate many underlying conditions, the doctor will check your overall medical condition, especially the heart and cardiovascular system, for any abnormalities. Blood may be drawn for laboratory analysis of any undisclosed maladies, such as high cholesterol, diabetes, and any liver or kidney disorders.

Candidates should expect to undergo drug screening. While the courts have ruled that preemployment drug testing for civilian positions represents an unwarranted intrusion into one's privacy, they have exempted the public sector from this restriction. The logic here is that corrections serves such a critical function in society that it demands the highest degree of trust and integrity from its employees. Remember, the goal of the selection process is to place only the best, most qualified, and extremely competent people in a position of public trust.

Polygraph Testing

The polygraph or lie detector is not as formidable as some people might think. The machine registers galvanic skin response, fluctuations in heart rate, blood pressure, and respiration patterns in response to inquiries from the examiner. Most people become quite anxious when the examiner puts the electrodes in place. That is to be expected. Once the testing begins, though, this anxiety lessens and the examiner can establish a baseline.

Expect this portion of the selection process to last around an hour. The operator will ask a general series of questions and will probe several specific areas. One question, for example, may be "Have you ever stolen anything of value from an employer?" Subjects may rack their brains trying to form a totally honest response. Suppose, for instance, that one night after you got off from work, you realized that you placed a company pen in your pocket instead of leaving it at the store. If you answer yes to this inquiry, the examiner will give you an opportunity to clarify what you mean. Obviously, putting a pen or pencil in your pocket is not exactly the kind of major transgression that will disqualify you from further consideration.

Agencies can be very particular about prior drug use. Some departments will not accept any applicants who admit to smoking marijuana in their youthful days. Other agencies, however, take a more understanding approach. Suppose, for example, that you experimented with marijuana two or three times in high school and then decided you did not enjoy the experience and gave it up. Some agencies may overlook this breach as an episodic part of growing up. Very frequent or heavy use, or any other chemical dependency for that matter, will jeopardize one's application.

In light of this, what should a person do if he or she tried marijuana a few times but then refrained from such usage? The best possible advice here is not to hide this fact. Instead, turn this situation to your advantage. Take the time to explain the circumstances behind this episode and emphasize that this behavior is in your distant past. Explain how the same conditions, such as peer pressure, no longer carry the ability to compromise your values. Bear in mind that corrections officers may handle numerous types and quantities of drugs and paraphernalia during the course of the job. Prospective employers want to be assured that you will be a trustworthy and upstanding employee who will live up to their expectations.

The Psychological Interview

If you have passed each of the earlier steps, the agency will contact you to arrange for an interview with a psychologist. The psychologist will have all your records available to him or her for review. The job of the psychologist is to probe and to determine whether the applicant would make a suitable corrections officer.

How does the psychologist do this and what is he or she looking for in a candidate? The psychologist will ask you a number of questions. Some of these items may include such things as why do you want to become a corrections officer, what would you do if you could not become a corrections officer, why is this career important to you, what do the people around you think about your career choice, what hobbies do you have, how do you spend your leisure time, what was the best movie you saw in the past year or so, and why do you think the agency should select you as a corrections officer.

In addition to listening to your responses, the psychologist will also be interested in your mannerisms. Eye contact, for example, is very important. Does the candidate look at the interviewer and maintain eye contact when it is appropriate? Does the person appear extremely nervous, squirm when presented with a difficult question, become easily intimidated, or seem unsure of himself or herself? Is the applicant too authoritarian or overbearing? Can this person balance the corrections aspects of the job with the rehabilitation components? Is there any indication that the interviewee is violence-prone?

The psychologist is looking for any signs that this person is ill-suited for the corrections role. The psychologist may pose a hypothetical set of circumstances and then ask how one would resolve the situation. In short, the psychologist will determine whether the candidate can adjust to the role, has the proper motivation for entering this career field, and if this person has the potential to be just and even-handed.

The Oral Interview

The final stage in the selection process is the oral interview. The oral board consists of a panel of raters who ask the candidate questions and then grade his or her responses. Ideally, this format allows the board to rank candidates in terms of how suitable they are for hiring.

The prospect of going before an oral board can be intimidating. However, a little bit of preparation can mean the difference between an awful experience and walking out of the room feeling confident. Two areas that are in your immediate control are your appearance and how you ready yourself for this meeting.

Somebody once said that first impressions are hard to erase. Well, you can turn that around to your advantage. The first piece of advice is to groom and dress yourself for success.

Male candidates should get a haircut prior to the interview. While you do not have to show up with a "zip" or a crew-cut, you do need to walk into the interview room looking as if you are serious about the job. Hair should not exceed the collar nor should it flow over the ears. A fresh shave is absolutely in order. While beards are out, it is okay to keep a mustache as long as it is neatly trimmed and does not extend beyond the corners of the mouth. Earrings are not becoming and fingernails should be cut and clean.

Female applicants should wear their hair in a reasonable length or come to the interview with their hair up in a businesslike fashion. Lipstick is appropriate as long as it is not purple, green, or any other outlandish color. Fingernails should be presentable. Glitter is taboo. Nail polish, like lipstick, should be subdued. Small earrings are an appropriate accessory. Multiple sets of earrings are out.

Both male and female candidates should minimize the amount of jewelry. A watch is fine, but a ring on each finger is not. Bracelets are distracting because they can make annoying sounds when gesturing or when placing hands on the table in front of you. Necklaces are out for men, but a simply styled one may be very suitable for women.

Men should wear a neatly pressed pair of pants along with a blazer or sports jacket. A suit would be even more impressive. A long-sleeved white or a light blue shirt, topped off with a subdued tie, rounds out the clothing. Remember, this is not the time to make a fashion statement by wearing a wildly colored shirt or a neon tie. The outfit should be finished with dark socks and polished shoes.

Women should follow a similar protocol. Business attire, such as a plain-colored skirt or pants and a jacket, is a must. A long-sleeved blouse should round out the appearance. Nylon stockings, either natural or dark-colored, are a necessity. Shoes should be polished and reasonable. High heels are not acceptable, especially if they are open-toed.

Make sure you arrive early. You should anticipate some difficulty with traffic, parking, and finding the exact location of the interview room. Also, by getting there early, you will have the opportunity to find a rest room and freshen up a bit. Comb your hair. Straighten out your jacket. Apply a tiny amount of perfume or cologne, but not so much that you overpower the interviewers.

Also pay some attention to the accessories that you carry. Both male and female candidates should consider carrying a briefcase or an attaché case. Should a female candidate be inclined to carry a purse, it should be dark, very plain, and appropriately sized. By the way, bubble gum or chewing tobacco are not acceptable.

The second area within your control is the preparation you make prior to the interview. What do you think is going to happen once the interview begins? What kinds of questions should you anticipate? How will you answer them?

Contrary to what many people think, your interview actually begins the moment the door opens and you step inside the room. More than likely, the highest ranking member on the board will introduce you to the other panelists. Think, for a moment, about how are you are going to handle yourself. Are you simply going to wave at each person on the board or are you going to go down the line and shake hands with them? Shaking hands is recommended. Once the introductions are over, the senior member will guide you to your spot, usually a chair. Do not sit down in the chair until you are invited to do so and, by all means, do not take off your jacket in order to feel more comfortable. Maintain a certain amount of decorum.

How do you think this session will begin? The board recognizes that you are nervous and a bit on edge. More than likely, the senior member will open the interview with a few comments and ask you to tell the panelists something about yourself. Here is your chance. Take this opportunity to distribute a fresh copy of your resumé to each person on the board. Remember, the panel will meet with a dozen applicants each day. Do something that distinguishes you from the rest of the crowd.

What will you say in your opening statement? What highlights should the board be aware of? What do you want them to notice about you? Make the assumption that nobody has read your file and that they are seeing you for the first time. What do you want them to focus upon in terms of your accomplishments and achievements?

What these questions hint at is your preparation prior to the actual interview. Try to guess what the board will ask and prepare your responses. Start out by making a list of everything you think you should include and then practice, practice, practice. This is your last chance to demonstrate why you deserve a job over anybody else.

What else do you think the panel may ask? One sure safe bet is that somebody will ask why you want to become a corrections officer. What are you going to say? Another question that may come up is what are the best and worst things that people can say about you. Be ready to explain why the agency should hire you over anybody else. A simple "yes" or "no" response will not suffice. Have a number of reasons or items that you wish to include at your disposal.

More than likely, the board will close by inviting you to ask the panel any questions if you wish. Mundane questions, like what time does check-on begin or what the starting salary is, should be avoided. (Salary information is listed in the advertisement or the requirements sheet that accompanies the application.) Instead, you may wish to inquire about how long it will take the agency to notify you of the results or if the board has any suggestions for how to improve your application.

Evaluating the Offer

Suppose for the moment, that two agencies extend you a job offer. Which one should you take? How should you arrive at your decision?

Obviously, you need some basic information in order to evaluate the offers. Assuming that the pay is roughly the same, you may want to inquire about what type of a package comes with each job. For example, will the agency provide all the equipment to new employees, including a vest, leather, and service weapon? What about life insurance, medical benefits, pension, vacation, overtime, and other items? Can officers hold off-duty jobs? Is there a tuition reimbursement plan for employees who go back to school and take courses?

A second area of consideration is the agency itself. What does it take to get promoted to the next rank? Is there a handsome pay increase that accompanies a promotion? How many openings will materialize in the next few years? After spending three to five years on the front line, will you have the opportunity to take on different assignments in other specialized units? Will the agency allow you to attend various training courses sponsored by FDLE so you can earn more incentive money?

As you can see, there are a number of variables to consider when making this career choice. But, if you have come this far, chances are you have the drive and energy to do well. Good luck!

APPENDIX A

LIST OF FLORIDA COUNTY SHERIFF'S OFFICES

The most informative website regarding Florida Sheriff's Offices can be found at the Florida Sheriff's Associate website (http://www.flsheriffs.org).

Alachua County Sheriff's Office
2621 SE Hawthorne Road
Gainesville, FL 32641
(352) 367-4000
http://www.co.alachua.fl.us/~acso/index.html

Baker County Sheriff's Office
56 North Second Street
MacClenny, FL 32063-2296
(904) 259-2231
http://www.sheriffsoffice.co.baker.fl.us

Bay County Sheriff's Office
3421 N. Highway 77
Panama City, FL 32405-5009
(850) 747-4700
http://www.panamacity.com/government/bayso

Bradford County Sheriff's Office
P.O. Box 400
Starke, FL 32091-0400
(904) 966-2276

Brevard County Sheriff's Office
700 Park Avenue
Titusville, FL 32780-4095
(321) 264-3201
http://www.sheriff.co.brevard.fl.us

Broward County Sheriff's Office
2601 W. Broward Blvd.
Fort Lauderdale, FL 33312
(954) 831-8900
http://www.sheriff.org

Calhoun County Sheriff's Office
342 East Central Avenue
Blountstown, FL 32424-0342
(850) 674-5049

Charlotte County Sheriff's Office
7474 Utilities Road
Punta Gorda, FL 33982-2417
(941) 639-2101

Citrus County Sheriff's Office
One South Park Avenue
Inverness, FL 34450-4994
(352) 726-4488
http://www.sheriff.citrus.fl.us

Clay County Sheriff's Office
P.O. Box 548
Green Cove Springs, FL 32043-0548
(904) 284-7575
http://www.claysheriff.com

Collier County Sheriff's Office
3301 East Tamiami Trail, Bldg. J
Naples, FL 34112
(941) 774-4434
http://www.colliersheriff.org

Columbia County Sheriff's Office
226 North Marion Street
Lake City, FL 32055-3933
(904) 752-9212

DeSoto County Sheriff's Office
208 East Cypress Street
Arcadia, FL 34226-4410
(863) 993-4700
http://www.desotosheriff.com

Dixie County Sheriff's Office
P.O. Box 470
Cross City, FL 32628-0470
(352) 498-1220

Escambia County Sheriff's Office
P.O. Box 18770
Pensacola, FL 32523-8770
(850) 436-9630
http://www.escambiaso.com

Flagler County Sheriff's Office
1001 Justice Lane
Bunnell, FL 32110
(386) 437-4116

Franklin County Sheriff's Office
270 State Road 65
Eastpoint, FL 32328
(850) 670-8519

Gadsden County Sheriff's Office
P.O. Box 1709
Quincy, FL 32353-1709
(850) 627-9233
http://www.sheriffsoffice.net

Gilchrist County Sheriff's Office
9239 South U.S. Highway 129
Trenton, FL 32693-5463
(352) 463-3410

Glades County Sheriff's Office
P.O. Box 39
Moore Haven, FL 33471-0039
(941) 946-0845

Gulf County Sheriff's Office
P.O. Box 970
Port St. Joe, FL 32456
(850) 227-1115
http://www.gulfcosofl.com

Hamilton County Sheriff's Office
P.O. Drawer A
Jasper, FL 32052-0541
(904) 792-1001

Hardee County Sheriff's Office
900 East Summit Street
Wauchula, FL 33873
(863) 773-0304
http://www.hardeeso.com/default.htm

Hendry County Sheriff's Office
P.O. Box 579
LaBelle, FL 33935-0579
(863) 674-4060

Hernando County Sheriff's Office
P.O. Box 10070
Brooksville, FL 34603-0070
(352) 754-6830
http://www.hcso.hernando.fl.us

Highlands County Sheriff's Office
P.O. Box 71
Sebring, FL 33871-0071
(863) 385-5111
http://strato.net/~sheriff

Hillsborough County Sheriff's Office
P.O. Box 3371
Tampa, FL 33601-3371
(813) 247-8000
http://www.hcso.tampa.fl.us

Holmes County Sheriff's Office
211 North Oklahoma Street
Bonifay, FL 32425-2296
(850) 547-3681

Indian River County Sheriff's Office
4055 41st Avenue
Vero Beach, FL 32960-1808
(561) 569-6700
http://www.ircsheriff.org

Jackson County Sheriff's Office
P.O. Box 919
Marianna, FL 32446-0919
(850) 482-9624

Jacksonville Sheriff's Office
501 E. Bay Street
Jacksonville, FL 32202-2975
(904) 630-2120
http://www2.coj.net./jso/default.htm

Jefferson County Sheriff's Office
Route 1, Box 31
Monticello, FL 32344
(850) 997-2523

Lafayette County Sheriff's Office
P.O. Box 227
Mayo, FL 32066-0227
(904) 294-1222

Lake County Sheriff's Office
360 West Ruby Street
Tavares, FL 32778-3877
(352) 343-2101

Lee County Sheriff's Office
14750 Six Mile Cypress Parkway, SE
Fort Myers, Florida 33912
(941) 447-1200
http://www.sheriffleefl.org

Leon County Sheriff's Office
2825 Municipal Way
Tallahassee, FL 32304
(850) 922-3300
http://www.lcso.leon.fl.org

Levy County Sheriff's Office
P.O. Drawer 1719
Bronson, FL 32621-1719
(352) 486-5111
http://www.levyso.com

Liberty County Sheriff's Office
P.O. Box 67
Bristol, FL 32321-0067
(850) 643-5615

Madison County Sheriff's Office
107 South Range Street
Madison, FL 32340
(850) 973-4151

Manatee County Sheriff's Office
515 11th Street West
Bradenton, FL 34205-7727
(941) 747-3011
http://legal.firn.edu.sheriff/manatee

Marion County Sheriff's Office
P.O. Box 1987
Ocala, FL 34478-1987
(352) 732-8181
http://www.sheriff.marioncountyfl.org/default.htm

Martin County Sheriff's Office
800 Southeast Monterey Road
Stuart, FL 34994-4507
(561) 220-7000
http://www.martin.fl.us/govt/co/sher

Monroe County Sheriff's Office
5525 College Road
Key West, FL 33040
(305) 296-2424
http://www.keysso.net

Nassau County Sheriff's Office
50 Bobby Moore Circle
Yulee, FL 32097
(904) 225-0331
http://www.ncso.net

Okaloosa County Sheriff's Office
1250 Northin Parkway
Shalimar, FL 32579
(850) 651-7400
http://www.sheriff-okaloosa.org

Okeechobee County Sheriff's Office
P.O. Drawer 1397
Okeechobee, FL 34973-1397
(863) 763-3117
http://www.sheriff.co.okeechobee.fl.us

Orange County Sheriff's Office
P.O. Box 1440
Orlando, FL 32802
(407) 836-3700
http://www.myweb.magicnet.net/ocso

Osceola County Sheriff's Office
400 Simpson Road
Kissimmee, FL 34744-4455
(407) 348-2222
http://www.osceolasheriff.org

Palm Beach County Sheriff's Office
3228 Gun Club Road
West Palm Beach, FL 3340
(561) 688-3000
http://pbso.org

Pasco County Sheriff's Office
8700 Citizen Drive
New Port Richey, FL 34654-4499
(727) 847-5878
http://www.pascocounty.com/sheriff

Pinellas County Sheriff's Office
P.O. Box 2500
Largo, FL 33779-2500
(727) 582-6200
http://www.co.pinellas.fl.us/sheriff

Polk County Sheriff's Office
455 North Broadway Avenue
Bartow, FL 33830-3998
(863) 533-0444
http://www.polksheriff.org

Putnam County Sheriff's Office
P.O. Drawer 1578
Palatka, FL 32178-1578
(904) 329-0800
http://www.putnamsheriff.org

Santa Rosa County Sheriff's Office
P.O. Box 7129
Milton, FL 32572-7129
(850) 983-1100
http://www.srso.net

Sarasota County Sheriff's Office
P.O. Box 4115
Sarasota, FL 34230-4115
(941) 951-5800
http://www.legal.firn.edu/sheriff/sarasota

Seminole County Sheriff's Office
100 Bush Blvd.
Sanford, FL 32773
(407) 665-6600
http://www.seminolesheriff.org

St. Johns County Sheriff's Office
4015 Lewis Speedway
St. Augustine, FL 32095
(904) 824-8304
http://www.co.st-johns.fl.us/const-officers/sheriff

St. Lucie County Sheriff's Office
4700 West Midway Road
Fort Pierce, FL 34981
(561) 462-7300
http://www.stluciesheriff.com

Sumter County Sheriff's Office
P.O. Box 188
Bushnell, FL 33513-0188
(352) 793-0222
http://www.sum.net/sumterso

Suwannee County Sheriff's Office
Suwannee County Courthouse
200 South Ohio Avenue
Live Oak, FL 32060
(904) 362-2222
http://www.alltel.net/~altonwms

Taylor County Sheriff's Office
County Courthouse
Perry, FL 32347
(850) 584-4225
http://www.firn.edu:80/sheriff/taylor

Union County Sheriff's Office
Union County Courthouse, Room 102
Lake Butler, FL 32054
(904) 496-2501
http://www.lake-butler.com/sheriff.htm

Volusia County Sheriff's Office
P.O. Box 569
DeLand, FL 32721-0569
(904) 736-5961
http://www.volusia.org/sheriff

Wakulla County Sheriff's Office
15 Oak Street
Crawfordville, FL 32327
(850) 926-7171
http://www.wcso.org

Walton County Sheriff's Office
72 North 6th Street
DeFuniak Springs, FL 32433-1944
(850) 892-8111
http://www.wcso-fl.com

Washington County Sheriff's Office
1293 Jackson Avenue, Bldg. 400
Chipley, FL 32428-0626
(850) 638-6111

APPENDIX B

LISTING OF CORRECTIONAL FACILITIES

To apply for a position, submit a State of Florida Employment Application to the regional or institutional personnel office where you desire employment. You may obtain a State of Florida Application from any of the offices listed or contact the website that the Department of Corrections maintains (http://www.dc.state.fl.us).

CENTRAL OFFICES

2601 Blair Stone Road
Tallahassee, FL 32399-2500
(850) 488-5021

REGION I:

2980 State Correctional Road
Marianna, FL 32448
(877) 209-2599

REGION II:

Route 7, Box 900
Lake City, FL 32055
(877) 724-2360

REGION III:

7504 Laurel Hills Road
Orlando, FL 32818

REGION IV:

5610 N. 9th Avenue
Ft. Lauderdale, FL 33309
(877) 724-2364

MAJOR INSTITUTIONS

REGION I:

Apalachee Correctional Institution East (Male)
35 Apalachee Drive
Sneads, FL 32460-0699
(850) 593-6431 or Suncom 786-1011

Apalachee Correctional Institution West
52 West Unit Drive
Sneads, FL 32460
(850) 593-6431 or Suncom 786-1011

Bay Correctional Institution (Male)
5400 Bayline Drive
Panama City, FL 32404
(850) 769-1455

Calhoun Correctional Institution (Male)
19562 S.E. Inst. Drive, Unit 1
Blountstown, FL 32424
(850) 674-5901 or Suncom 787-2010

Century Correctional Institution (Male)
400 Tedder Road
Century, FL 32535
(850) 256-2600

Gadsden Correctional Facility (Female)
P.O. Box 390, Hwy. 12
Quincy, FL 32353-0390
(850) 875-9701

Gulf Correctional Institution (Male)
500 Ike Steele Road
Wewahitchka, FL 32465-0010
(850) 639-1000 or Suncom 790-1000

Holmes Correctional Institution (Male)
3142 Thomas Drive
Bonifay, FL 32425-0190
(850) 547-2100 or Suncom 781-1397

Jackson Correctional Institution (Male)
5563 10th Street
Malone, FL 32445-3144
(850) 569-5260 or Suncom 778-1101

Jefferson Correctional Institution (Male)
1050 Big Joe Road
Monticello, FL 32344-0430
(850) 997-1987 or Suncom 285-1300

Liberty Correctional Institution (Male)
HCR 2 Box 144, County Road 1641
Bristol, FL 32321-9711
(850) 643-2141 or Suncom 788-1011

Madison Correctional Institution (Male)
Route 4, Box 2695
Intersection Hwy. 14 & County Road 360
Madison, FL 32340
(850) 973-5300 or Suncom 296-5300

Okaloosa Correctional Institution (Male)
3189 Little Silver Road
Crestview, FL 32539-6708
(850) 682-0931 or Suncom 672-1011

Quincy Correctional Institution (Male) Annex
2225 Pat Thomas Parkway
Quincy, FL 32351
(850) 627-5400 or Suncom 212-5400

Santa Rosa Correctional Institution (Male)
5850 East Milton Road
Milton, FL 32583
(850) 983-5800 or Suncom 689-5800

Wakulla Correctional Institution (Male)
110 Melaleuca Drive
Crawfordville, FL 32327
(850) 421-0777 or Suncom 299-0777

Walton Correctional Institution (Male)
691 WW II Veteran's Lane
DeFuniak Springs, FL 32433
(850) 892-6141 or Suncom 692-1300

Washington Correctional Institution (Male)
4455 Sam Mitchell Drive
Chipley, FL 32428-3597
(850) 773-6100 or Suncom 784-6100

REGION II:

Baker Correctional Institution (Male)
P.O. Box 500, U.S. 90
Lake Basin Road
Sanderson, FL 32087-0500
(386) 719-4500 or Suncom 885-4500

Columbia Correctional Institution (Male)
Route 7 Box 376
U.S. 90
Lake City, FL 32055-8767
(386) 758-8090 or Suncom 850-8090

Cross City Correctional Institution (Male)
P.O. Box 1500
Veteran's Road
Cross City, FL 32628-1500
(352) 498-5576 or Suncom 629-1011

Florida State Prison (Male)
7819 N.W. 228th Street
Raiford, FL 32026-1000
(904) 368-2500 or Suncom 830-2500

Gainesville Correctional Institution (Male)
2845 N.E. 39th Avenue
Gainesville, FL 32609-2668
(352) 955-2001 or Suncom 625-2001

Hamilton Correctional Institution (Male)
10650 S.W. 46th Street
Jasper, FL 32052-1360
(386) 792-5504 or Suncom 872-5504

Lake City Correctional Facility (Male Youth)
Route 7, Highway 90 East, Box 1000
Lake City, FL 32055
(386) 755-3379

Lancaster Correctional Institution (Male Youth)
3449 S.W. State Road 26
Trenton, FL 32693-0158
(352) 463-4100 or Suncom 640-4100

Lawtey Correctional Institution (Male)
7819 N.W. 228th Street
Raiford, FL 32026-2000
(904) 782-3811 or Suncom 859-1011

Mayo Correctional Institution (Male)
P.O. Box 448
U.S. Hwy. 27 North
Mayo, FL 32066-0488
(904) 294-4500 or Suncom 829-4500

New River Correctional Institution (Male)
7819 N.W. 228th Street
Raiford, FL 32026-3000
(904) 368-3000 or Suncom 830-3000

North Florida Reception Center (Male)
P.O. Box 628
Hwy. 231
Lake Butler, FL 32054-0628
(386) 496-6000 or Suncom 883-6000

Putnam Correctional Institution (Male)
128 Yelvington Road
East Palatka, FL 32131
(386) 325-2857 or Suncom 867-1011

Taylor Correctional Institution (Male)
8501 Hampton Springs Road
Perry, FL 32348
(850) 838-4136 or Suncom 295-4136

Union Correctional Institution (Male)
7819 N.W. 228th Street
Raiford, FL 32026-4000
(386) 431-2000 or Suncom 831-2000

REGION III:

Avon Park Correctional Institution (Male)
P.O. Box 1100
County Road 64 East
Avon Park, FL 33826-1100
(863) 453-3174 or Suncom 745-6183

Brevard Correctional Institution (Male Youth)
855 Camp Road
Cocoa, FL 32927-3709
(407) 634-6000 or Suncom 362-6000

Central Florida Reception Center (Male)
7000 H. C. Kelley Road
Orlando, FL 32831-2518
(407) 207-7777 or Suncom 343-7777

Hernando Correctional Institution (Female Youth)
16415 Springhill Drive
Brooksville, FL 34604-8167
(352) 754-6715 or Suncom 663-6715

Hillsborough Correctional Institution (Male Youth)
11150 Highway 672
Riverview, FL 33569-8402
(813) 671-5022 or Suncom 512-0264

Lake Correctional Institution (Male)
19225 U.S. Highway 27
Clermont, FL 34711-9025
(352) 394-6146 or Suncom 634-1324

Lowell Correctional Institution (Female)
P.O. Box 147
3269 N.W. 105th Street
Lowell, FL 32663-0147
(352) 622-5151 or Suncom 653-1417

Marion Correctional Institution (Male)
P.O. Box 158
3269 N.W. 105th Street
Lowell, FL 32663-0158
(352) 401-6400 or Suncom 667-6400

Polk Correctional Institution (Male)
10800 Evans Road
Polk City, FL 33868-6925
(863) 984-2273 or Suncom 588-1241

Sumter Correctional Institution (Male)
P.O. Box 667
County Road 476B
Bushnell, FL 33513-0667
(352) 793-2525 or Suncom 633-1000

Tomoka Correctional Institution (Male)
3950 Tiger Bay Road
Daytona Beach, FL 32124-1098
(386) 323-1070 or Suncom 380-1070

Zephyrhills Correctional Institution (Male)
2739 Gall Boulevard
Zephyrhills, FL 33541-9701
(813) 782-5521 or Suncom 535-1100

REGION IV:

Broward Correctional Institution (Female)
20421 Sheridan Street
Ft. Lauderdale, FL 33332
(954) 252-6400 or Suncom 430-6400

Charlotte Correctional Institution (Male)
33123 Oil Well Road
Punta Gorda, FL 33955
(941) 575-2828 or Suncom 746-1200

Dade Correctional Institution (Adult Female)
19000 S. W. 377th Street
Florida City, FL 33034-6409
(305) 242-1900 or Suncom 478-1900
Annex: (305) 242-1700 (Adult Male)

DeSoto Correctional Institution (Male) Annex
13617 S.E. Highway 70
Arcadia, FL 34266
(863) 494-3727 or Suncom 766-7100

Everglades Correctional Institution (Adult Male)
1601 S.W. 187th Avenue
Miami, FL 33185
(305) 228-2000 or Suncom 479-2000

Glades Correctional Institution (Male Youth)
500 Orange Avenue Circle
Belle Glade, FL 33430-5222
(561) 996-5241 or Suncom 237-1011

Hardee Correctional Institution (Male)
6901 State Road 62
Bowling Green, FL 33834-9505
(863) 773-2441 or Suncom 757-1200

Indian River Correctional Institution (Male Youth)
7625 17th Street S.W.
Vero Beach, FL 32968
(561) 564-2795 or Suncom 240-2812

Martin Correctional Institution (Male)
1150 S.W. Allapattah Road
Indiantown, FL 34956-4397
(561) 597-3705 or Suncom 249-5011

Moore Haven Correctional Facility (Male)
P.O. Box 718501
1900 East State Road 78 N.W.
Moore Haven, FL 33471
(863) 946-2420

Okeechobee Correctional Institution (Male)
3420 N.E. 168th Street
Okeechobee, FL 34972
(863) 462-5474 or Suncom 761-5474

South Bay Correctional Facility (Male)
600 U.S. Highway 27 South
South Bay, FL 33493
(561) 992-9505

South Florida Reception Center (Male)
P.O. Box 02-8538
14000 N.W. 41st Street
Miami, FL 33178
(305) 592-9567 or Suncom 475-0200

WORK CAMPS, FORESTRY CAMPS, AND ROAD PRISONS

REGION I:

Berrydale Forestry Camp (Male)
6920 Highway 4
Jay, FL 32565
(850) 675-4564 or Suncom 671-4142

Calhoun Work Camp
19562 S.E. Inst. Drive, Unit 2
Blountstown, FL 32424
(850) 674-2887 or Suncom 787-2421

Caryville Work Camp (Male)
P.O. Box 129
1005 Waits Avenue
Caryville, FL 32427-0129
(850) 548-5321 or Suncom 771-4620

Century Work Camp
400 Tedder Road
Century, FL 32535
(850) 256-2600

Franklin Work Camp (Male)
1001 West Highway 98
Apalachicola, FL 32320-1272
(850) 653-8500 or Suncom 771-2127

Graceville Work Camp
5230 Ezell Street
Graceville, FL 32440
(850) 263-9230

Gulf Forestry Camp (Male)
3222 DOC Whitfield Road
White City, FL 32465
(850) 827-7412 or Suncom 771-2045

Holmes Work Camp
3182 Thomas Drive
Bonifay, FL 32425
(850) 547-2703 or Suncom 781-1397

Jackson Work Camp
5607 10th Street
Hwy. 71 North
Malone, FL 32445-9998
(850) 569-5260 or Suncom 778-1410

Liberty Work Camp
HCR 2, Box 144
Bristol, FL 32321-0711
(850) 643-3330 or Suncom 788-1011

Madison Work Camp
P.O. Box 692
Intersection Hwy. 14 & County Road 360
Madison, FL 32341-0692
(850) 973-5334 or Suncom 296-5334

Okaloosa Work Camp
3189 Little Silver Road
Crestview, FL 32539-6708
(850) 682-0931 or Suncom 672-1117

River Junction Work Camp
300 Pecan Lane
Chattahoochee, FL 32324-3700
(850) 663-3366 or Suncom 289-3304

Tallahassee Road Prison (Male)
2628 Springhill Road
Tallahassee, FL 32310-6730
(850) 488-8340 or Suncom 278-8340

Walton Work Camp
301 World War II Veterans Lane
DeFuniak Springs, FL 32433
(850) 892-6141 or Suncom 692-1300

REGION II:

Baker Work Camp
P.O. Box 500
U.S. 90
Sanderson, FL 32087
(904) 719-4670 or Suncom 885-4670

Columbia Work Camp
Route 7, Box 378
Lake City, FL 32055-8767
(386) 758-8090 or Suncom 850-8090

Cross City Work Camp
P.O. Box 1500
Veteran's Road
Cross City, FL 32628-1500
(352) 498-5576 or Suncom 629-1330

Florida State Prison W/C
P.O. Box 747
State Road 16
Starke, FL 32091-0747
(904) 368-2500 or Suncom 830-2500

Gainesville Work Camp (Male)
1000 N.E. 55th Blvd.
State Road 26 East
Gainesville, FL 32609
(352) 955-2045 or Suncom 625-2045

Hamilton Work Camp
10650 S.W. 46th Street
Jasper, FL 32052
(904) 792-5409 or Suncom 872-5409

Lancaster Work Camp
3449 S.W. SR 26
Trenton, FL 32693
(352) 463-4100 or Suncom 640-4130

Mayo Work Camp
P.O. Box 1805
Hwy. 27
North Mayo, FL 32066
(904) 294-2335 or Suncom 829-4752

REGION III:

Avon Park Work Camp
P.O. Box 1100
County Road 64
East Avon Park, FL 33826
(863) 453-3174 or Suncom 745-6176

Brevard Work Camp
855 Camp Road
Cocoa, FL 32927-3700
(407) 634-6130 or Suncom 362-6130

Largo Road Prison (Male)
5201 Ulmerton Road
Clearwater, FL 34620-4091
(727) 570-5135 or Suncom 513-5135

Levy Forestry Camp (Female)
P.O. Box 1659
County Road 343
Bronson, FL 32621-1659
(352) 486-5330 or Suncom 645-5330

Marion Work Camp
P.O. Box 227
3269 N.W. 105th Street
Lowell, FL 32663
(352) 401-6400 or Suncom 667-6863

Lowell CI Boot Camp
P.O. Box 147
3269 N.W. 105th Street
Lowell, FL 32663
(352) 622-5151 or Suncom 653-1325

Polk Work Camp
10800 Evans Road
Polk City, FL 33868-6925
(863) 984-2273 or Suncom 588-1473

Sumter Boot Camp
P.O. Box 667
9544 County Road 476B
Bushnell, FL 33513-0667
(352) 793-2525 or Suncom 633-1000

Sumter Forestry Camp
P.O. Box 1807
9544 County Road 476B
Bushnell, FL 33513-0667
(352) 793-2525 or Suncom 633-1000

Tomoka Work Camp
3950 Tiger Bay Road
Daytona Beach, FL 32124-1098
(904)323-1221 or Suncom 380-1222

REGION IV:

Arcadia Road Prison (Male)
2961 N.W. County Road 661
Arcadia, FL 34266
(863) 993-4628 or Suncom 740-4628

Big Pine Key Road Prison (Male)
P.O. Box 430509
450 Key Deer Blvd.
Big Pine Key, FL 33043
(305) 872-2231 or Suncom 451-5105

Fort Myers Work Camp (Male)
P.O. Box 051107
2575 Ortiz Avenue
Fort Myers, FL 33994-1107
(941) 332-6915 or Suncom 748-6915

Glades Work Camp
2600 N. Main Street
Belle Glade, FL 33430
(561) 996-0149 or Suncom 237-1011

Hardee Work Camp
6899 State Road 62
Bowling Green, FL 33834-9505
(863) 773-2441 or Suncom 757-1200

Hendry Work Camp
12551 Wainwright Drive
Immokalee, FL 34142
(941) 657-3654 or Suncom 734-1104

Loxahatchee Road Prison (Male)
230 Sunshine Road
West Palm Beach, FL 33411
(561) 791-4760 or Suncom 242-4760

Martin Work Camp
1150 S.W. Allapattah Road
Indiantown, FL 34956
(561) 597-3705 or Suncom 249-5262

WORK RELEASE CENTERS

REGION I:

Marianna WRC (Male)
2980 State Correctional Road
Marianna, FL 32448
(850) 482-9532 or Suncom 789-9532

Panama City WRC (Male)
3609 Highway 390
Panama City, FL 32405
(850) 872-4178 or Suncom 777-4178

Pensacola WRC (Male)
3050 North L Street
Pensacola, FL 32501
(850) 595-8920 or Suncom 695-8920

SHISA–West (Female)
416 West Virginia Street
Tallahassee, FL 32301
(850) 222-4859

Tallahassee WRC (Male)
2616A Springhill Road
Tallahassee, FL 32310
(850) 488-2478 or Suncom 278-2478

REGION II:

Dinsmore WRC (Male)
P.O. Box 62208
13200 Old Kings Road
Jacksonville, FL 32219-2208
(904) 921-1700 or Suncom 833-1701

Lake City WRC (Male)
Route 8, Box 1604-C
Lake City, FL 32055
(386) 758-0535 or Suncom 885-0535

Santa Fe WRC (Male)
2901 Northeast 39th Avenue
Gainesville, FL 32602-1202
(352) 955-2070 or Suncom 625-2070

SHISA–East (Male)
2830 Park Street
Jacksonville, FL 22205
(904) 389-1303

REGION III:

Bartow WRC (Male)
550 N. Restwood Avenue
Bartow, FL 33830-4200
(863) 534-7037 or Suncom 515-0642

Cocoa WRC (Male)
585 Camp Road
Sharpes, FL 32927
(321) 690-3210 or Suncom 362-3210

Daytona Beach WRC (Male)
3601 U.S. Highway 92 West
Daytona Beach, FL 32124-1002
(904) 238-3171 or Suncom 380-3210

Kissimmee WRC (Male)
2925 Michigan Avenue
Kissimmee, FL 32744
(407) 846-5210 or Suncom 327-5210

Orlando WRC (Female)
7300 Laurel Hill Road
Orlando, FL 32818
(407) 578-3510 or Suncom 326-3510

Pine Hills WRC (Female)
7504 Laurel Hill Road
Orlando, FL 32818
(407) 578-3514 or Suncom 326-3514

Pinellas WRC (Female)
5205 Ulmerton Road
Clearwater, FL 33760-4002
(727) 570-5138 or Suncom 513-5138

SHISA–South (Male)
6017 S.E. Robinson Road
Belleview, FL 34475
(407) 690-3210

St. Petersburg WRC (Male)
4237 8th Avenue, South
St. Petersburg, FL 33711-2000
(727) 893-2289 or Suncom 513-9118

Tarpon Springs WRC (Male)
566 Brady Road
Tarpon Springs, FL 34689-6707
(813) 942-5420 or Suncom 513-5420

REGION IV:

Fort Pierce WRC (Male)
1203 Bell Avenue
Ft. Pierce, FL 34982
(561) 468-3929 or Suncom 240-3929

Hollywood WRC (Male)
P.O. Box 8759
8501 W. Cypress Drive
Pembroke Pines, FL 33025
(954) 985-4720 or Suncom 473-4720

Atlantic WRC (Female)
263 Fairgrounds Road
West Palm Beach, FL 33411
(561) 791-4187 or Suncom 242-4187

Miami North WRC (Male)
7090 Northwest 41st Street
Miami, FL 33166
(305) 470-5580 or Suncom 429-5580

Opa Locka WRC (Male)
5400 Northwest 135th Street
Opa Locka, FL 33054
(305) 827-4057 or Suncom 481-4057

Pompano WRC (Male)
5600 Northwest 9th Avenue
Ft. Lauderdale, FL 33309
(954) 958-5510 or Suncom 423-5510

West Palm Beach WRC (Male)
261 West Fairgrounds Road
West Palm Beach, FL 33411
(561) 791-4750 or Suncom 242-4750

Pineapple Press publishes a full line of books about Florida. Check our website at www.pineapplepress.com. Call us at 800-PINEAPL (800-746-3275) or write us at P.O. Box 3889, Sarasota, FL 34243 to send you a complete catalog. Other books you might be interested in include:

Study Guide to the Florida Law Enforcement Officer's Certification Examination (New Edition) by William Doerner and Charles Rushing. Hundreds of practice questions modeled after those on the actual exam, along with concise tips on registration, procedure, test-taking, exam results. Also detailed information on seeking employment after passing the exam. ISBN 1-56164-109-X.

Everglades Lawmen: True Stories of Game Wardens in the Glades by James T. Huffstodt. Today's game wardens chase escaped convicts, keep surveillance on drug runners, and recover wreckage from plane crashes as well as arrest deer, turkey, and alligator poachers. Meet the men and women who dedicate their lives to protecting the only Everglades on earth. ISBN 1-56164-192-8.

Florida Law: A Layman's Guide (Third Edition) by Gerald B. Keane. A practical, readable guide to your legal rights in Florida. Indispensable for anyone who needs to know the basics of Florida law. ISBN 1-56164-187-1.

The Exploring Wild Florida series is a set of comprehensive guidebooks to the natural areas and wildlife that abound in Florida. *Exploring Wild North Florida* by Gil Nelson, ISBN 1-56164-091-3. *Exploring Wild Northwest Florida* by Gil Nelson, ISBN 1-56164-086-7. *Exploring Wild South Florida* by Su Jewell, ISBN 1-56164-262-2.

A Florida Cattle Ranch by Alto "Bud" Adams Jr. and Lee Gramling. The story of one cattle ranch as well as the story of one state, one way of life, and one family's stewardship of the land. ISBN 1-56164-159-6.

The Springs of Florida by Doug Stamm. Descriptions, maps, and beautiful all-color underwater photos of Florida's many springs, which include the deepest and largest known in the world. ISBN 1-56164-054-9.

Poisonous Plants and Animals of Florida and the Caribbean by David W. Nellis. Each poisonous plant and toxic animal is described and illustrated with color photos. Also includes in-depth information on symptoms and treatments. ISBN 1-56164-111-1 (hardcover) and ISBN 1-56164-113-8 (softcover).

NOTES

NOTES

NOTES